W9-CRY-394

"Whether you're an experienced salesperson or someone just entering the workforce, *The Golden Apple* provides a wealth of strategies that will guide you to success in your career."

—Michael A. Alicea
Senior Vice President, Human Resources, VNU Business Media

"Kathy gives you the sum total of what you need to know to build a lifetime of long-term and dynamically loyal relationships."

—Gale Hollingsworth
Western Regional Sales Director, *Black Enterprise* magazine

"Here is your blue ribbon guide to success in business and life."

—Jim Casella
Vice Chairman, Reed Business Information

"Kathy Aaronson at eight developed 'kid courage,' which she's used to create 'Sales Athletes' and a business empire. This book is smart and sensitive; we're fortunate that Kathy's so sharing of herself with us. I urge everyone interested in personal and career excellence to get into this fast and enjoyable read."

—William Becker
Chairman, Kodak Theatre/The Chicago Theatre

"Every bite the reader takes from *The Golden Apple* will nourish them with the motivation and action steps needed to fulfill their professional goals."

—Ron Wilcox
Executive Vice President and Chief Business and Legal Affairs Officer
Sony BMG Entertainment

"Sometimes do you feel you don't fit in? Kathy Aaronson's book will show you how to celebrate and market your uniqueness and value."

—Greta E. Couper, Ph.D.
Alumni Career Services, Pepperdine University

"Kathy Aaronson has captured the essence of what makes for success—knowledge, persistence, and the ability to 'read' people and respond to them in a positive and affirmative fashion."

—Peter A. Young
President, Digital Printing Systems, Inc.

"A perfect book for setting a positive and productive work culture. I'm buying copies for my entire sales team!"
—Anthony Andrade
National Advertising Manager, Dow Jones

"Here in one place are the ABCs to get you on the path to success and keep you moving in the right direction."
—Perry Grayson
Vice President—Western Region, Hachette Filipacchi Media

"I took a bite of Kathy Aaronson's *The Golden Apple* and can say people who read this book will gain knowledge in how to succeed in business. People with limited resources will be able to expand their horizons with this valuable book!"
—Steve Elish
Vice President/Group Publisher, Back Stage Publications

"Kathy Aaronson inspires me, and this book is a great extension of her amazing advice and counsel."
—Christie Barnes Stafford
Los Angeles Account Manager, *Wired* magazine
The Condé Nast Publications, Inc.

"In *The Golden Apple,* Kathy shares her skill in teaching others how to be sensitive to, and capitalize on, the opportunities around us all. Buy two or three copies, because once you read it, you'll pass it like a fine vintage to your best friends."
—Mel Snyder
Managing Director, ProClinical, Inc.

"In a time when the evolution of the media industry has created an environment of innovation-by-necessity, we're fortunate to have resources like *The Golden Apple* to rely on. Kathy Aaronson continues to light the way for business development professionals who look to raise the bar on behalf of their brands."
—Charles Weiss
National Advertising Director, *Back Stage* magazine

The Golden Apple

The Golden Apple

How to Grow Opportunity and Harvest Success

Kathy Aaronson

WILEY

John Wiley & Sons, Inc.

Published by John Wiley & Sons, Inc., Hoboken, New Jersey.
Published simultaneously in Canada.

The Sales Athlete® is a servicemark/trademark owned by Kathleen Aaronson.

Library of Congress Cataloging-in-Publication Data:

Aaronson, Kathy.
    The golden apple : how to grow opportunity and harvest success /Kathy Aaronson.
        p. cm.
    ISBN-13 978-0-471-77782-3 (cloth)
    ISBN-10 0-471-77782-X (cloth)
    1. Selling.   2. Customer relations.   3. Relationship marketing.
4. Consumer satisfaction.   5. Career development.   I. Title: How to grow opportunity
and harvest success.   II. Title.
    HF5438.25.A218 2006
    658.85—dc22   2005034538
Printed in the United States of America.

10   9   8   7   6   5   4   3   2   1

Dedicated to the thousands of generous mentors and teachers who guide and inspire us to meet our personal and professional best.

Contents

Contents

Contents

Acknowledgments

I am forever grateful to The Sales Athlete, Inc., senior management team: Thomas Mohler, Michelle Sebens, Lani Tedja, Carrie Meathrell, and Nicole Fealey—without their daily efforts I could never have spared the time needed to write *The Golden Apple*; and to Sam Means and Philip Slagter for creating the illustrations you see throughout *The Golden Apple*.

. . . many thanks to Peter Koechley and Jamie Temple for their contributions to the process.

. . . special thanks to Mary Tahan, our literary agent who valued *The Golden Apple* and found the perfect home for this project with Debra Englander, executive editor at John Wiley & Sons.

. . . and a very special thank you to Ann Bancroft, who helped me render my voice on these pages.

Introduction

As a child on a remote New Hampshire farm, I was so desperate for company that one day I took a tractor and drove it across a field toward the nearest neighbor, unaware that the field had been seeded and I was destroying everything in my path. My punishment wasn't too harsh, fortunately, but my parents were neither willing nor able to solve the problem of loneliness that led to my tractor escapade. They worked long, hard hours just to feed the family, so asking them for a bike or to be chauffeured to a friend's house was out of the question. I was only eight years old, but it was clear to me that if I wanted to meet people and get a taste of the world outside our little plot of land, I was on my own.

To pursue those dreams, I used the creativity and enthusiasm that children so often find easier to access than adults do. I call it "kid courage." My options were limited, but I made use of every one of them. If I was a girl stuck on a farm with no money, no bike, no friends, and no place to go, I would find a way to meet the people who passed by on the highway and earn money in the process.

I did it the way many children driven by a need for independence find the courage to become young entrepreneurs. But instead of turning lemons into lemonade, I found what was available on the farm that I was allowed to sell. To most of the world, that amounted to produce that, while fresh, was too bumpy, too unevenly colored, or too misshapen to be attractive enough for the grocer's shelves—in other words, "nonsaleable" produce. To me, however, these oddball fruits and vegetables became the currency that would enable me to meet people driving by in their cars. I just knew I'd be able to turn crooked carrots and bumpy tomatoes into freedom, connections, and cash. They were my Golden Apples. I set up a roadside produce stand and called it the Happiness Patch.

I wasn't aware of it at the time, but in the process of turning my produce stand into a successful enterprise, I was learning important lessons and building a foundation for a business philosophy that would serve me throughout my career. These were the very lessons I put into the service of training thousands of others to become successful professionals—people I call "Sales Athletes."

I learned that value is what you see, believe, and communicate. Even bumpy tomatoes and three-legged carrots are tasty and delicious; and if you understand and believe in that value, you can convey it to others.

It quickly became clear that I couldn't sell unless I found a way to get people to slow down long enough to see what I was selling. I learned the importance of creating "speed bumps" to slow people down and get their attention.

Once they've stopped, people really do respond to pretty packaging better than to a product simply sitting on a table. And the way I presented myself also played a role in how my product was received. I also learned that getting people to stop and getting them to buy are two different things, even if the package is perfect.

I believed in what I was selling. I knew I had good produce at good prices. That probably wasn't so obvious, though, to anyone looking at my cucumbers that appeared to be growing warts. I had to convince customers that this produce was as clean, fresh, tasty, and healthful as any they could buy in the store—and less expensive, too. I did so by telling them the stories of how the produce was grown and what my family did with it.

Over time I learned that there are different types of customers—but not that many different types—and that there was a way to create receptivity in each of them and leave them as satisfied customers. Most important, I learned that sales is about people and that giving something extra to every encounter will win long-term success and satisfaction in sales and in life.

Within a decade of my first weekend selling vegetables at the Happiness Patch, I boarded a Trailways bus and left home for the excitement and possibilities of New York City. I soon became one of the few women hired to sell advertising in a national magazine.

Knocking on the doors of Madison Avenue, I'd say, "Hi! I'm young, I'm single, and if you want to reach a girl like me, you'll find me reading *Cosmopolitan.*"

I found mentors—the most successful salespeople at the Hearst Publishing Company, the corporate owners of *Cosmopolitan*. These were the top salespeople at *Good Housekeeping*, *Harper's Bazaar*, *House Beautiful*, *Town and Country*, and *Eye* magazines. They were the kind of salespeople I would later describe as Sales Athletes.

In eleven years of selling advertising to sales managers, to marketing directors, and to presidents of some of the most successful corporations in the world, and also some of the least successful, I established an invaluable overview of how people sell. I met Sales Athletes in every major industry and learned that what set them apart from the many who struggle simply to stay afloat was not simply a matter of luck or training. Sales Athletes—the people who succeed despite economic downturns and who transcend barriers of age, gender, physical circumstance, or lack of academic credentials—have embraced a way of living and doing business that makes success easier than failure.

When I reached the point in my own career where employers were willing to pay me the equivalent of a year's salary for part-time work, I set out to share what I had learned about what makes Sales Athletes thrive. The philosophy and ethic of The Sales Athlete, Inc., is based on the lives of successful people who know how to seamlessly meld business and pleasure; who view training as a continuing process; and who nurture, expand, and maintain relationships through career changes and moves. Sales Athletes give something extra to every endeavor; and in the process, they are rewarded with career security and satisfaction.

The seed of my kid courage—the desire to connect with others—developed not only into my career, but also into a philosophy and strategy of career planning, coaching, and job placement that are built on the importance of relationships. At The Sales Athlete, Inc., and in training sessions nationwide, I coach others in a different way of looking for employment and career satisfaction. I encourage them to focus on the type of *people* they like working with, rather than on a field or a subject area that is familiar or attractive. I teach the skills for building positive business relationships and client loyalty that buffer a person's career through changes in the economy or industry and allow smooth transitions from one career arena to another. And when I come across those special people I call Sales Athletes—people who have motivation, passion, commitment to training, and the habit of always giving something extra—I mentor them and connect them with excellent employers who are my clients in search of top talent in the most lucrative and satisfying careers. Nothing is more satisfying than making these connections.

I'm sure you can dig back and remember a time when you used creativity and courage as a child to get what you wanted. At that moment, you might remember creating the currency of freedom and planting the seed of your future career choices.

Sadly, those skills we find in childhood—skills we don't recognize at the time as persuasion, negotiation, marketing—can lay dormant as we grow into adults, unless we nurture and develop them as carefully as a farmer does his crops. I call my company The Sales Athlete, Inc., because athletes are not born; they must train and stay in shape to succeed.

In this book I want to show you how to harvest your own kid courage—those strengths you exhibited as a child—to see and convey your value in a way that will help you weather uncertainty and economic change. You'll see how to turn the equivalent of bumpy vegetables into golden apples and start doing business in a way that will ensure your ability to make a living as long as you live— regardless of age, academic credentials, gender, religion, or physical circumstance.

Seeds planted at my childhood produce stand were nourished and developed throughout my career into an ethic and way of building and maintaining relationships, confidence, and skills. The lessons learned by an eight-year-old roadside entrepreneur have brought me success in life through economic booms and busts, changes in my industry, and seismic shifts in the marketplace and the world. They have served me well in my advertising and publishing career, and they continue to serve me and hundreds of my clients well today as I train, consult, and speak to people seeking career satisfaction and success. The program built on these lessons has facilitated into satisfying sales, marketing, advertising, and entertainment careers for thousands of floundering recent college graduates and hundreds of people making dramatic late-in-life career changes. It has taken and revitalized the careers of people who were standing still professionally during six deep, rolling consumer recessions, the end of the Vietnam War, Desert Storm, the dot-com crash, and September 11, 2001. These lessons will show you how career satisfaction and security are not dependent on your selection of industry or employer, but on the way you build and nurture relationships. They'll provide a roadmap for staying successful regardless of what's dealt to you by Mother Nature, a change in the law, technology, or world political climate.

In each chapter of this book, I share with you a lesson learned at that roadside stand and then describe how building on that lesson will serve to make you more credible, valuable, confident, and successful in your career. I encourage you to reach back and rediscover your own kid courage and to remember that time of childish ingenuity. Bring your kid courage along as you follow the lessons I am about to share with you—lessons that began when I was eight years old and that I have continued to learn and teach over three decades in executive search, training, and corporate coaching. Follow them, and you will find success to be easier than failure, in business and in life.

Part One

Bringing Out the Value Within

LESSON 1: A crooked carrot can be as valuable as a golden apple. To get what you want, you must first learn how what you have is of value to others.

LESSON 2: People have busy lives. If you want them to be receptive to your product, service, candidacy, or idea, you first need to create "speed bumps" to slow them down.

LESSON 3: To create receptivity with the greatest number of people, be prepared to do business in a way that makes them comfortable.

Chapter 1

Finding Worth, Providing Value

My early years were spent in rural New Hampshire on a small farm that barely supported our family. Every evening we'd gather around the dining room table to enjoy a meal made primarily from the fruits and vegetables grown on our own soil. Not the best-looking produce—that was reserved for sale at market—but the fresh, perfectly edible fruits and vegetables that were bumpy and misshapen and considered nonsaleable. Our crooked carrots, oddly shaped tomatoes, and unevenly colored squash would become stews and soups—what in those days was called "poor people food" but today is prized as healthy, delicious comfort cuisine: "heirloom" vegetables fresh from the farm.

While mealtimes were lively, I was a lonely eight-year-old. There were no neighbors in sight of our farm, only the cars that drove by with strangers in them, and I imagined those strangers must have fascinating lives and stories to tell.

On the wall of our dining room was a framed needlepoint quotation: "Let me live in a house by the side of the road and be a friend to man." It inspired in me countless childhood daydreams about meeting new people from exotic places. I was a child who desperately wanted to connect with others. We did live "by the side of the road"—on

Route 9 between Keene and Portsmouth—but in a place so remote it was extremely difficult to be a "friend to man."

One day when our family drove into town, I focused intently on the big, paper, grocery store signs advertising the same type of produce that we grew: "carrots, 10 cents a bunch," "tomatoes, 25 cents a pound." Meanwhile, I thought of how the type of "imperfect" produce we ate for dinner, just as healthy as that sold at the store, was often tossed on the compost heap or left in the ground.

Those odd-looking carrots and pretzel-shaped squash weren't valuable to the grocery store, where only "perfect" produce was sold. But I knew they would have value to people who would chop them into salads or soups, can them, or use them to make pies, because that's what we did with them. They were fresh and clean and came straight from the good earth. Why couldn't others also benefit from that value? I could save people the trouble of going into the store by making my produce accessible at the side of the road, and that would provide value, too. Surely I could convince people to pay half of what the grocery store charged and to feel lucky about the bargain. Suddenly, I saw a connection between those bumpy vegetables on our table and the needlepoint on the wall. In that moment, I found a way to satisfy my longing for new friends. These homely fruits and vegetables would become my Golden Apples.

Using as a display table a well-worn pruning table wheeled down to the side of the road, I set up a produce stand to sell this fresh, nutritious, nonsaleable produce from the farm. I called my stand the Happiness Patch because I knew it would provide me a way to become a friend to man.

Over time, my little wooden pruning table was up-graded to a larger, wooden telephone wire spool that had been left by the side of the road. The people driving by who wanted a quick snack for the road, who were looking for a place to stretch or to break up a monotonous drive, or who were looking for a "genuine country experience" became my customers. Many began to return to my little stand week after week. As the seasons passed, I learned that different customers were seeking different kinds of experiences at the Happiness Patch, and I improvised ways to please each type of customer who stopped by. In the process, I was learning how to determine what a customer values and how to convey that value to different types of customers.

I didn't realize it at the time, but in order to be successful at the Happiness Patch, I was developing criteria to determine the value of my misshapen produce to every type of customer that might stop by. Those criteria would in later years help me and hundreds of my clients determine the value of anything. I learned first at the Happiness Patch and confirmed later in my career that *determining value is the first step toward success in virtually every type of transaction and interaction, whether it's conveying an idea, navigating a negotiation, solving a problem, getting a job, cementing a relationship, or selling a product, a service, or an idea.*

Checklist: What Is Value?

1. Does it meet a demand?
2. Does it save time and/or effort?

3. Does it carry authority?
4. Does it convey credibility?
5. Does it provide value by association?
6. Does it offer a positive experience?

Meeting a Demand

My produce didn't meet the "perfect" test, but for bargain hunters like the two elderly ladies on fixed incomes who became my regular customers, it did meet a demand for food that was just as fresh and nutritious, but not as expensive, as the produce sold at the grocery store. I knew I would be able to sell it, because I knew its value to these customers.

> ### ↬ LESSON 1 ↫
>
> A crooked carrot can be as valuable as a golden apple. To get what you want, you must first learn how what you have is of value to others.

In today's rapidly changing, technologically complex world, it may seem difficult to determine and meet a demand. But you really don't need a team of market researchers to help you in this process. If you are realistic, are willing to think creatively, and trust in common sense, you'll find ways to meet a demand that may not be obvious to others. I have worked with many people who have turned adversity into success by determining a demand and filling it when others weren't.

Sales Athlete Michele Laven, director of Integrated Media and vice president of Clear Channel Radio, recalls her family's swimming pool business in Cleveland, Ohio. Hot summers and freezing winters limited the demand for their product to less than six months out of the year, so the family barely made a sale until her father figured out a way to meet a demand that fit his skills and inventory during the cold winter months: backyard winter wonderlands. Transforming bleak yards and their empty pools into dazzling landscapes with thousands of tiny lights and decorations, the family business not only filled a demand but also provided a way to keep in contact with customers all year long.

By adapting their business to the seasons, Michele and her family also recognized a truth that people in business ignore at their peril: *Demand isn't constant. It's up to you to adapt to the demand of the consumer or to create demand by offering something new.*

Rather than eking by until another summer came along, this enterprising businessman found a way to use his skills to create year-round demand.

In the same way that successful businesspeople recognize how to spot and meet a demand, they also adapt quickly to changes in the economy. A professional home chef in California, for example, had finally built his business to where dozens of regular clients demanded his home catering services, and dozens more were on a waiting list. When the dot-com boom went bust, however, his clients were quick to call and say they could no longer afford the hundreds of dollars a month he charged for the high-end meals they'd been ordering. Instead of simply accepting the loss of these clients, the chef quickly adjusted to the changing demand, switching from lobster and exotic mushroom dishes to meatloaf and delicious stews. Not only was he able to lower his prices, but he offered less extravagant packages of once a week, rather than a minimum of three times a week. His newly unemployed clients, along with several from his waiting list, were grateful for the less expensive comfort food. This chef made it through a trying time that put many of his peers out of business.

Sometimes, you can create a demand simply by reminding people of what they need. Every spring in my apartment building, just before the summer heat sets in, an air-conditioning service notifies the building that they'll be coming through the building on a specific date to change filters and do a routine check of the air-conditioning systems. The company charges a set price to each apartment scheduling a visit on that day. Now, of course the company would also come to the building a dozen different times if a dozen apartment owners each called separately and arranged appointments to have their systems checked. But by announcing "We're coming through on this date" (with a "take it or leave it" implicit in the one-day-only offer), the service creates a demand. And by scheduling a day to change everyone's filters, the company has provided value in a second important way—and this leads to my second criteria.

Saving Time and Effort

By saving customers the time and effort of scheduling their own appointments, the air-conditioning service was providing value. The same principle applies at convenience stores, where the promise of a quick and painless transaction, with no long line or miles of shelves to navigate, trumps the savings of buying an item at lower cost at a supermarket. Why do you buy prepared granola instead of making your own? Time and effort saved. Certainly I can wait for my husband or myself to have the time and inclination on a weekend to rake the leaves in our yard. But if an enterprising teen sees the demand and offers to save us time and effort by knocking on my door with a rake in his hand, I'll pay him money on the spot to do the job.

Carrying Authority

I may have been only eight years old when I started out in business at the Happiness Patch, but I carried the authority of one who had helped to plant, fertilize, harvest, and clean the produce I sold. I could say with authority, "This type of squash holds up well and tastes delicious in vegetable soup. We enjoyed some just last night." I could show my customers the field where the produce was grown, and I could name the day it was dug from the ground or picked from the vine.

People pay for authority because buying from an expert saves money and time in the long run. Knowing that a product, service, or idea is backed with the mastery and expertise of an authority provides the buyer or listener with confidence and security. Making yourself an authority or working to become an expert in your field automatically provides value. How many times have you heard or experienced the frustration of a customer at a warehouse store trying to make a choice on a piece of electronic equipment? When the salesperson has no idea about the difference between products or even how various features work, the customer loses confidence and is often ready to pay a premium to buy from someone who's an authority on the merchandise.

There are fewer jobs for generalists today than for people who have claimed a niche and developed solid expertise. People who have followed their bliss—steeping themselves in the subjects they love—have managed to create professions that are both satisfying and lucrative, because they convey both authority on the subject and joy in their work. An authority who provides a valuable, specialized service can transcend a lack of academic credentials, age discrimination, or economic downturns. Employees who develop themselves into the indispensable go-to person for a specific issue area are much more likely to have success and security in their careers.

Conveying Credibility

Credibility comes with authority, but it also must be conveyed in the way you present yourself, your product, your service, or your idea. If you were considering plastic surgery, for example, would you feel comfortable if the surgeon explaining the procedure had the letters "L-O-V-E" tattooed on his fingers and a six-month training certificate on his wall? At the Happiness Patch, I conveyed credibility because I understood and believed in the value of my produce. I was polite, wore clean clothes, and was clearly eager to serve. I could show customers exactly where and how my fruits and vegetables were grown.

I once knew a man who was for many years a superb consultant, but who refused to wear a suit. His "trademark" outfit was a safari hat with its strap hanging under his chin, an aloha shirt, cargo shorts, and sandals. This man was truly an expert, and people in the field valued his expertise. But it was widely known he never went as far as he could have because a first impression would convey the idea that he was a wild card. Don't forget that your appearance, speech, manners, and personality can convey credibility, and credibility has marketable value. By choice, you should never wear anything that diminishes the power of the message you are there to convey.

Value by Association

Association is one of the things people are buying when they purchase a status symbol, join a country club, or support alumni organizations. It's what gives us peace of mind when we see the Good Housekeeping Seal of Approval or the AAA logo. Does your product, service, or idea convey something people want to be associated with? Which people? There's value in providing a sense of association with others. Determining and providing positive associations will help you win receptivity to your product, service, or idea. The Happiness Patch, for example, was only a tiny produce stand, but its association with our family farm brought it credibility. People buying my vegetables felt connected to the earth, to the farm, and to a rural way of life.

Offering a Positive Experience

When customers came to the Happiness Patch, they weren't only there to buy bumpy vegetables. The experience of stopping by a family farm to buy fresh-from-the-earth produce from an earnest little girl was simply more enjoyable for them than buying the same vegetables from the supermarket, even if our vegetables weren't perfect. My produce stand carried positive associations for people, and for some it became part of a treasured routine. It is hard to overestimate the value of offering a positive experience. People pay more to go to their neighborhood grocer not only for the convenience but also because it is the place where they're known and are likely to run into friends and neighbors. I've placed many Sales Athletes in jobs that offer less compensation up front than an alternative offer might because of the prospect of a more enjoyable work environment and more compatible coworkers.

Nothing is of more obvious value than a product or

service that *feels* good. Women pay hundreds of dollars for spa treatments they could do far less expensively at home, because it feels more relaxing and pleasant to be pampered by another person. On the other hand, if the manicurist cuts your cuticle or the masseuse leaves you with aches you didn't have when you first lay on her table, all value is gone, and your relationship with that business is *over*. Why would anybody buy anything from a company if it doesn't feel good?

Anytime you have an idea to convey or a product or service to sell, run it through the checklist for determining value. Does it meet a demand? Save time or effort? Carry authority? Convey credibility? Provide value by association? Offer a positive experience? You'll be prepared to convince others only when you have determined all the ways you have to offer value.

Nothing Happens Until You Sell Yourself

Before you can convince any listener, whatever his or her needs, that what you have is of value, you must first see and believe in and be able to convey your own value. Why? Because you are the first thing your listener sees or hears. Nothing happens until you can sell yourself.

Don't forget to use the checklist for determining value on pages 14 and 15 to remind yourself of what *you* have to offer your listener, customer, or prospect.

Where are you in demand? Has technology or other

changes created new places and ways for you to provide value?

During the darkest days of the economic slump in 2001, many laid-off middle managers came to my placement service hoping to find jobs. The typical job seeker was frightened and frustrated. Often past middle age but not ready for retirement, they found their positions had suddenly been outsourced, eliminated through down sizing, or moved elsewhere in a merger. While I was able to find jobs for some of them, most often I advised these job seekers not to seek a job but to fill a demand that was growing outside of the traditional workforce. Because of the economic downturn, jobs were scarce, but *work* remained plentiful. The companies forced to lay off workers still had a demand for projects to be managed, but they did not have the ability to make long-term hiring commitments.

Once these job seekers thought creatively about their own value to potential employers and looked realistically at the job market and economy, they were able to fill a demand consistently and well. In the process, they updated and expanded skills and contacts, putting themselves in a better position for long-term employment. Many have also found that filling a demand through project work can provide as much income and satisfaction as a long-term, full-time job.

Technology may have changed the landscape when it comes to what consumers demand, but it has also made it possible to meet demand in creative new ways. If you are willing to continually update your skills, technology will offer you the ability to reach and provide value to a much broader audience. Technology can also help you move past ageism and other prejudices, but if you fail to develop technological skills, you risk becoming a dinosaur even if you are still in your twenties.

I worked with a woman who found herself disabled with severe diabetes, who was no longer able to go into her job every day as a clerk in the vital records office of a county. So, being both realistic and creative, she found another way to meet a demand for skills she had honed through years in public service. Today, she makes a better income and more satisfying living with an online records search business run out of her home, finding and having delivered to lawyers records they need in lawsuits, negotiations, and employment searches.

When determining where you are in demand, think about all the types of people and businesses who might find value in your skills, product, service, or idea. Then list how those people would use your skills, product, service, or idea. You might think of nontraditional ways of filling a demand and, in doing so, create a successful market for what you have to offer. Ask yourself these questions:

How can you save people time and effort?

You'll have a receptive audience only if you make it immediately clear to potential customers or clients that you will not steal their precious time. Instead, let them know early in your presentation how you will *save* them time and effort.

What expertise do you have that lends you authority?

While a license, degree, or certification conveys expertise, so do years of experience in your career, numbers of clients satisfied with your service, and the level of demand for your speaking, teaching, or mentoring skills. All of these are part of a hard-won career, and you should not hesitate to list them all on a resume or in a scrapbook that chronicles your career accomplishments. In today's rapidly changing workplace, maintaining expertise requires a commitment to continual training and updating of skills. Your value to prospective clients or employers increases when you can demonstrate both a solid foundation of experience and an eagerness to stay on the cutting edge.

In what ways are you credible?

At The Sales Athlete, Inc., I put my credibility on the line by offering a "satisfaction guarantee with no fine print." It's simple, it's powerful, and I stand behind it. I can offer guaranteed satisfaction because I know what I'm doing and I know the value of my service and the results it provides. When placing a candidate in a job, I work with the employer to do a complete breakdown of the job description so that every aspect of that job will be understood. There are no surprises to the new employee, and I only place someone who is qualified to do every aspect of that job with the skill and enthusiasm of a Sales Athlete. You, too, can offer a guarantee of satisfaction if you carefully research the needs of your client and understand completely how your product, service, or idea will fit your client's needs. Businesses as varied as Costco and Nordstrom have built business on satisfaction guarantees, and the goodwill and loyalty such policies buy far outweigh the rare occasions when someone might abuse it. You can also build credibility by being active in your community. Serve on boards, volunteer your services to non-profit organizations, and give back in ways that reflect well on you and the work you do.

Are you professional in the way you present yourself?

The way you dress, speak, and behave in all situations should create receptivity in the people you meet.

What associations do you have that lend you credibility?

Mine your contacts and think of what associations you have that lend you credibility and authority. Whether you can claim leadership in a community organization, membership in an alumni association, military service, religious affiliation, or membership in a service club, remember that these associations lend you credibility and authority and provide a level of comfort to your customer or listener. Associations also provide connections with others that are automatic icebreakers: "I went to State University, too. What years were you there?"

In what ways do you offer a positive experience?

Perhaps nothing is as important in determining your value as someone to trust and do business with than to *be* a trustworthy, likeable communicator. In his bestseller *Blink* (Little, Brown, 2005), Malcolm Gladwell describes research findings that doctors who make their patients *feel* cared for are rarely sued for malpractice, even when they have made critical mistakes in patient care. On the other hand, I've known people in business who have excellent skills, an impeccable resume, and other strong points, yet they consistently fail to succeed because of a negative attitude that leaves potential clients wanting to flee from their presence.

If a client, customer, or listener walks away from an encounter with you feeling enriched, you are much more likely to develop a positive, ongoing business relationship that will be satisfying to you both.

In the same vein, CEOs and human resources managers of companies I deal with know that to attract Sales Athletes, a company must create a culture where people leave the office each day believing they are worth more than when they walked in that morning. That outcome means a culture that values balance, continued training, a spirit of vitality, and the need to replenish daily—all as a way of living and doing business.

Different people will perceive in a variety of ways your value and the value of the product, service, or idea you are trying to sell. So your understanding of who buys what and how (Chapter 3) also will add value to all of your encounters in business.

Once you have determined your own value, and once you believe in what it is you want to do or to have happen, you have determined your destiny. You'll soon know how to deal with those people and factors that stand in your way, and nothing will stop your progress!

Chapter 2

Slowing Down
the Traffic

I opened for business at the Happiness Patch much as any child would set up a lemonade stand. I wiped off the big wooden spool at the bottom of the road leading to the farm, and I put two boxes of fresh, clean, bumpy, misshapen produce on top. And I waited. I was excited about the connections I'd soon make with those people whizzing by in their big, beautiful, shiny cars.

It didn't take long for disappointment to set in, however, because those cars just continued to drive by as I stood there for hours. I'd smile and even wave at the cars, and not a single driver stopped to buy my vegetables. To pass the time, I'd color in the map of the United States, filling in a state with a different color each time a license plate from that state would pass me on the road. Once in a great while, a car would pass, then stop and back up to see what I had for sale—or even if I had something for sale, which wasn't clear from the boxes. After a few days of this, my teacher stopped by, curious as to how I was doing.

"Kathy," she said, gently, "you need some signs so people will know what you're doing here."

Back at school, Miss August took me to the auto shop teacher, who helped me make five big, heavy plywood signs. On each we painted a vegetable. One depicted an apple, but it could double as a tomato, depending on the season. Another pictured a cucumber that could double as a pickle. There was a carrot. Then a sign that read, "Fresh Produce—¼ mile," and another, to be placed just ahead of the curve in the road: "Happiness Is Just Around the Corner."

Those signs were taller than I was, and nearly as heavy, but I lugged them down the road and planted them about a quarter mile apart.

Suddenly, the cars began to slow down. Drivers' curiosity was piqued, their interest raised. In retrospect, I believe once they turned the corner and saw it was a little girl selling those fresh, clean, marketed-for-a-mile vegetables, they slowed down to a stop. My vegetable signs weren't just signs, they were speed bumps, slowing people down enough to give them time to think about, then act on, their desire to buy my produce.

Until I posted my speed bumps, the potential customers driving down that two-lane road weren't prepared to stop to look at my little stand. They were mesmerized by the scenery or lost in their thoughts or conversations. Even if they had a positive thought about the little girl and her vegetable stand, by the time that thought

registered, they'd already driven by. My speed- bump signs slowed them down.

The first one caught their attention. The second slowed them down.

The third caused them to consider what I was selling.

The fourth built on that interest.

And the fifth promised a pleasurable experience.

It took a lot of effort to create those signs—much more effort than just setting up a stand and waiting for someone to stop by. But the effort put into slowing down the traffic paid off. After five speed bumps, drivers felt a subtle obligation to stop and buy produce from my stand, *before they even got out of their cars.*

〜 LESSON 2 〜

People have busy lives. If you want them to be receptive to your product, service, candidacy, or idea, you first need to create "speed bumps" to slow them down.

In today's deal-a-minute world, multiple distractions are everywhere. It's harder than ever before to cut through all the noise and hold someone's attention long enough to be receptive to your product, service, candidacy, or idea. That's why it is more important than ever to build speed bumps into every transaction. People are simply not going to stop their busy lives to listen to what you have to offer, no matter how beneficial your idea may be to them. It's your job to create the speed bumps that will catch their attention, slow them down, preset their receptivity, and create a subtle sense of obligation to listen to what you have to offer. Speed bumps can be used not only to slow down traffic that's coming your way, but to forge new relationships with people who aren't yet aware you exist.

I was just eighteen years old when I found my way to New York City, working at an ad agency and running an antique stand on the weekends. One day an advertising salesman from *Cosmopolitan* magazine called on me and let it slip that his salary was twice as much as my combined earnings. That did it. Very few women, and particularly not young women, were being hired those days in the highly competitive world of major media advertising sales, but I *knew* I had what it took to do the job. After all, I *was* the Cosmopolitan Girl—young, single, fashion-conscious, independent. I managed to get an interview, and I thought it went well. Then I waited and waited to hear whether I would be hired. And as I waited for the phone to ring, it was beginning to feel like those first few days at the produce stand. Remembering the advice of my first mentor, the teacher who taught me the value of speed bumps, I decided to take the initiative and create five speed bumps—the same number as I'd used to slow down drivers before they got to the Happiness Patch—to land the job I wanted. I needed to create a first bump that would be noticed, a second that would slow them down in their process enough for them to consider me, a third that would engage their interest, a fourth that would lead them to want to know more, so that by the fifth—when I actually met them again face-to-face—they would be asking, "When can you start?"

Stopping in at Dunhills, the famous cigar store in Manhattan, I bought four "It's a Girl!" cigars and had each individually wrapped in a black patent leather box with a gold ribbon. I sent them, one at a time—staggered like my roadside signs—to the publisher of *Cosmopolitan* magazine who I hoped would hire me. The first box arrived with a card that said, "It's a girl!" Nothing more. No signature, just the cigar inside. The next day, there came the patent leather box and the cigar, with a note that said, "And she's

35

a *Cosmo* girl!" On day three: "And her name is . . ." Then I skipped a day before delivering the fourth and final cigar with a card reading: "Kathy Aaronson!"

I got the job—over, I was told, about two hundred others who had also applied, most of them with experience in advertising.

Speed bumps create receptivity whether you're seeking a job, running for office, selling a product or service, or seeking acceptance of your project or idea.

Creating Prospects

Doing business with speed bumps is the antitheses of the old-fashioned "grab what you can get" sales strategy, where you get someone on the phone, start telling them about what you have to offer, and just hope to gain some traction. At The Sales Athlete, Inc., I don't place, train, or consult people in that style of marketing because it is disrespectful of people's time and needs and it turns people off. Therefore, it is both the least satisfying and least effective way of marketing. Instead, Sales Athletes develop speed bumps to create receptivity with people who want, need, or could benefit from their product, service, or idea. This amount of time and effort may seem like a lot at the outset, just to preset a sale. But when effective speed bumps are put in place, the transaction that ensues is much more likely to be easy and pleasurable and to develop into a long-term, satisfying business relationship.

In fact, the actual process of selling is short and sweet when the energy is placed into the preplanning of setting receptivity. It's important to use enough speed bumps to slow listeners down, catch their attention, have them consider the value of your idea to their business or their life, and then allow themselves to be receptive to hearing your offer or your idea. Sales Athletes say it "takes five 'touches' to make a touchdown," and that summarizes the speed-bump strategy.

The Five-Touch Technique

To be effective, speed bumps must be consistent and tell a story. They should cause your listener to notice, slow down enough to pay attention, become interested, and want to hear more. Once you've established rapport and built credibility in those four steps, the fifth step should create receptivity to hearing your proposal.

Here's how I use speed bumps to reach a busy, successful executive:

First: A note or postcard: "Dear Thomas, I have an idea that I believe will benefit you, and I promise not to waste a single minute of your time. I will call your assistant to set up an appointment to go over my idea with you."— Kathy Aaronson, CEO, The Sales Athlete, Inc.

Second: A call to Thomas's assistant, with essentially the same message left on her voice mail, adding, "Of course Thomas is the best judge, but I really think my idea would save time and effort and generate profit. This only requires a minute, and I promise if you recommend he spends that minute, I will not waste a single moment of his time."

Third: An e-mail to the assistant, following up: "Just following up on the voice mail I left earlier: I have an idea I really believe will benefit Thomas. I won't waste a single minute of his time, and if you'd be kind enough to recommend he speak with me, I promise you'll be happy that you did."

Fourth: CC (carbon copy) Thomas on the e-mail to the assistant.

Fifth: Call Thomas. The message is brief and consistent, the tone professional, enthusiastic, helpful: "I hope you received my card and my message. I do have an idea I think would be a great fit for your business. Of course, only you can judge that, but if you'll give me just a minute to outline my idea, I promise I won't waste a moment of your time."

Now, some sales experts say *never* leave a voice-mail message; wait until you reach the prospect in person and can put him or her on the spot to respond. I wholeheartedly disagree. Voice mail is a great speed bump. It gives you an opportunity to preset the potential customer to be receptive to your idea. It allows the listener to hear your voice and to recognize you as professional, courteous, brief, and respectful, *without* putting the listener on the spot or obligating him or her to do anything but listen to the message.

By the time I actually have five minutes scheduled for a face-to-face meeting with Thomas, he is receptive to hearing my idea. I've made it clear I respect his judgment, and that judgment may turn out to be that my idea is not useful. But because I believe it *is* beneficial to Thomas and because my speed bumps have preset him to be receptive, the chances of an open dialog and a successful transaction are greatly improved.

See how putting the effort into speed bumps pays off? Even if Thomas doesn't judge this particular idea to be in his best interest, I have gained an opportunity to present my business and myself to him as credible and professional. The meeting will be pleasurable, and he will likely be a receptive contact in the future. When you have put speed bumps in place, the darkest outcome is one where you've established a rapport that allows you to circle back again with another idea.

Using speed bumps help you move past the fear of rejection in sales and increases the likelihood your idea will be heard. Because they know it takes an average of five speed bumps, or five "touches" to make a touchdown, Sales Athletes are not disappointed when the first touch doesn't work. If a sale occurs after fewer than five speed bumps, it's considered a lucky day.

Failure to use speed bumps leads people to work in jobs they don't like and to be unsuccessful in careers when they are capable of excelling. I can't tell you the number of smart, talented people I've counseled who approach job hunting like this: See a job advertised; imagine, after reading the one-paragraph description, that it would be a good job; send a resume; hope someone will call and hire them! That failure to use speed bumps—first to determine whether the job is worth pursuing in the first place, then to preset the employer to be interested in an interview and hiring—is the reason so many people live long, hard days with little satisfaction. The same goes for people who experience failure in getting their ideas accepted on the job, in making sales, and even in establishing personal relationships. When you are interested in an outcome that requires the receptivity of someone else, you have a much greater chance at success if you preset his or her interest.

Ironically, lack of confidence and fear of rejection is what keeps many people from taking the extra steps at the outset of selling an idea, candidacy, product, or service—when taking those steps actually instills confidence and lowers the likelihood of rejection.

Speed bumps can be verbal—notes, e-mails, voice messages—or they can be what I call "premium"—inexpensive but thoughtful items that simply and cleverly catch the recipient's attention. Premium speed bumps not only deliver your message, they signal to the recipient: "I care about you enough to have put some thought into this. I'm not here to bother you; I'm going to give you something back for your time." If, for example, a client prospect brusquely rejects your first telephone call or visit, follow it up with a second speed bump that he or she will remember.

Some examples I've used with great success: A lottery ticket taped to my calling card, along with the message: "Take a chance!" Or a car windshield guard that will keep the interior of the recipient's car cool and that pulls out with a message about how to best use my services. In the wintertime, I've sent inexpensive one-cup coffeemakers, with my business card and motto affixed to the handle. If it's the holiday season and your client prospects are swamped, think of sending along a candy cane in a red cellophane wrapper with a heart sticker. The message: "Let's take a few minutes and I'll show you an idea to help parlay the profits of this holiday season into a more profitable Valentine's Day" (or February).

When I have an hour between appointments, I go on speed-bump safaris, looking for little items that will serve as effective entrees to prospective clients. These little items fill a large desk drawer, because I never know when I might use one and which will best fit the business I want to reach. One of my perennial favorites is the blue-ribbon-winner button that fits into an envelope and conveys a winning idea. Another is the miniature "message in the bottle," with a message inside tailored to the client. When I cold-called the owner of a group of Lexus dealerships, attached to my calling card was a tiny, metal, toy Lexus—his gatekeeper whisked me in within seconds. Speed bumps can help you get through to a client even at times of crisis, when most businesses simply aren't returning calls. One such time was when the United States first went to war in Iraq, during the buildup and execution of Operation Desert Storm. Business simply halted as managers worried how long the war would last and how it might affect the world and the U.S. economy. They simply weren't placing orders, buying ads, hiring, or building. At one prestigious, old-line accounting firm, clients had dwindled disastrously, and even the few remaining clients weren't returning calls. When it became clear that running into business associates at the country club was no longer working as a way of maintaining and building its client base, the firm called me to train them in new ways of breaking through.

I stood before the room full of buttoned-down executives, held up the front page of the *Los Angeles Times*, and said, "On today's front page is a photograph of George Bush [the elder, U.S. president at the time]. I want you to cut it out, paste it onto a piece of paper, and paste onto that a caption that says, 'My friend George believes it is important we connect as quickly as possible.' And then sign it."

With that, the senior partner of this firm stood up, said, "I hope no one's paying her!" and stalked out of the room, offended that anyone would have his firm consider such a concept. Nobody else left, however; and two days later, the senior partner was asking his secretary, "Where's that picture of George Bush?" Every one of the CPAs in the firm who'd used the "George wants us to connect" speed bump had their calls returned. (Shortly afterward, I received a memo from the senior partner, saying, "I'd like you to know that you and my friend George helped us to connect with clients at a critical time in our firm. . . .")

Most important was the message those CPAs sent in their third speed bump, delivered over the phone or in person: What "George" wanted clients to know was that he did *not* intend the country to shut down because of the war. To support our country, it was important to keep doing business.

Speed bumps breaking through in crisis times can serve not only to deliver business opportunities but also to help companies through the crisis itself. When the events of September 11, 2001, brought the country to a standstill, it quickly became clear that unless people pulled themselves out of their deep sadness and got back to business, the victims of the disaster would include countless people laid off and businesses shut down in a radius of thousands of miles from the World Trade Center. Nobody was buying, nobody was moving. It was ghastly.

At that point, I really felt corporations had a moral obligation to continue to transact business. If they didn't, businesses that had let tragedy paralyze their workplaces would end up terminating employees, adding further to the victims of this national disaster.

I turned to "messages in a bottle" to get my message across—small plastic bottles with scrolls inside on which you can write your own message. They come with an address sticker and just need a fifty-five cent stamp to be ready to pop right into the mailbox. (Shortly after 9/11, I bought a case of a dozen, then called the 800-number on the bottle and ordered another twelve dozen of them.)

On the scroll I put a quote from an editorial that had run in *Adweek* magazine, about Kathy Aaronson being a "little known treasure of Southern California." And I added the message, "I believe it's very important we connect, because without training in how to move through this extraordinary period in American history and business, you will have to terminate employees and ultimately they, too, will be victims."

I proceeded to call each company I'd sent the messages to, and even in that chaos, my calls were taken by each of them, if they hadn't already called me. I put together a presentation on what to say to companies to get them to transact business.

I was willing to reach out with my premium offer because I believed in the message: Managers needed to be shaken out of their post-9/11 state of shock because they had a moral obligation to lead. Those businesses did shake themselves out of inaction and avoided layoffs. As a result, the businesses remain loyal clients to this day.

Sometimes, when there's no time to spread speed bumps out over days or weeks, the use of creative premiums can combine five bumps into one or two powerful messages. One of my clients was in charge of selling advertising for *USA Weekend* and wanted to contact packaged-goods advertisers for a special recipe issue. As life would have it, her deadline was short, and the deals had to be closed quickly. She found and purchased some wooden boxes with sliding tops, very nicely done, and inside those boxes placed a cake mix, a wooden spoon, a miniature whisk, and a recipe, along with a reminder that the closing date for the recipe issue of *USA Weekend*—read by one of every five Americans every Sunday—was right around the corner. Those boxes contained all five speed bumps. Once she contacted the advertisers, all she had to do was state the facts and close on what would be one of the most successful recipe issues ever.

I've seen time and time again how creative use of premium speed bumps can break through disinterest or distraction and put a Sales Athlete ahead of the competition. One of my favorite examples is a twenty-something young woman who'd landed a job with a company marketing to teenaged girls—a company that was number five in a four-company field. Her task was to land six fifty-thousand-dollar national accounts, in a market where success had eluded every one of her predecessors.

Clearly, knocking on the same doors with the same old message was not going to knock her competitors out of the box. So this young woman developed an ingenious first speed bump. She lined six, six-by-four-by-four-inch boxes with festive packaging "grass" and into each placed an inexpensive trinket emblematic of teenaged girls: a small plastic hair dryer, a bar of strawberry-scented soap, a tiny handbag. Above that was placed a laminated storybook held together with a simple ring clasp. In clever pictures, charts, statistics, and graphs, it told the story of the lucrative teen market: how much disposable income thirteen-to-sixteen-year-old girls have, how much they spend on the client's product each year, how often they come into contact with the business she represents.

With that investment of thirty-six dollars per client, that young woman opened the doors to every one of those accounts. She quickly became the top salesperson in her company and within a few short years was able to start a publishing company of her own.

Of course, sensitivity must be used when choosing premiums to use as speed bumps. Misused, they can offend rather than attract clients or, worse, foreclose your chance of ever doing business with the prospective customer. One salesman I know made the egregious error of giving a gift of a cashmere sweater to a fashion buyer—something that would have gotten the buyer fired had she accepted it. I wouldn't send a lottery ticket to anyone I might suspect would be offended by gambling or invite someone to a meal unless we'd already met and established a potential business relationship. *Caution: Always be certain that your premiums reflect good taste and professionalism, clearly state your message, and reflect well on the image of your company.*

The test of an effective speed bump is this: After it is received, does it create a *subtle* obligation to listen to the person who sent it?

Speed bumps are everywhere, and once you become conscious of what they are, you'll start noticing how they work to cut through the clutter and noise of daily life by creating a buzz of their own. You'll realize that many of the spontaneous purchases or decisions you make aren't really that spontaneous at all, but the result of speed bumps causing you to be receptive. Just recently I was walking briskly and purposefully down the grocery aisle, picking up only the items on my list. A red plastic dispenser sticking out of the aisle, with a coupon sticking out of it, caught my attention. I pulled a coupon and discovered it was for the item right above the dispenser—a bag of shelled walnuts. Suddenly, I was holding a coupon for fifty cents off the regular price of a product I absolutely, positively would not have bought. And it was the only item in the entire aisle that I looked at, turning the package to check for salt content. That speed bump nailed me! Within a minute I'd noticed, considered, appreciated, then decided: "Healthy, salt-free, fifty cents off, I'll try it!"

I don't believe in selling people what they don't need or want. My strategies are geared to creating satisfaction by providing what others want and need and building relationships in the process. I use speed bumps to help determine the receptive audience. Once I have slowed a person down enough to get their attention, I can say, "May I ask you a couple of questions to see if this will be a good fit for you?" And that allows me to determine how my service will be of value to the listener.

Take the extra time and effort up front to put speed bumps in place. By the time you actually present your idea, you'll be dealing with a receptive audience ready to benefit from what you have to say.

Chapter 3

Why We Buy, and How

Once I had set up my stand and began slowing traffic enough to get drivers interested in stopping, I figured that selling to one person would be the same as selling to the next. Doesn't everyone buy in the same way? Don't people just decide what they want, what they are willing to pay, and then either purchase an item or walk away? What I learned as the weeks went by is that customers aren't all alike. If I wanted to see my customers more than once and have them tell others about my stand, I had to learn how to deal with different types of buyers in different ways.

My sign promised: "Happiness Is Just Around the Corner." But I soon learned that what creates happiness and receptivity in some buyers doesn't make all buyers happy or receptive.

One type of customer would get out of his car, stretch his legs, say a brief hello, and toss me a quarter for a dime's worth of produce. He wasn't interested in being shown where the produce was grown or discussing the merits of different grape varieties. This person wasn't unpleasant; he was just someone ready to zero in on something fresh to eat, pick it up, and be on his way, never to be seen again. It might have been an entertainer on his way to the Portsmouth Naval Yard, stopping to buy a bunch of grapes for the road, or a traveler from another state, out looking at the fall colors and with hours to go before lunch or dinner. I'd never see these people again, and I didn't get to know too much about them, but they were quick and easy buyers.

Another type of customer would pull up to the stand every Sunday, unloading kids from the back seat to break up their weekly Sunday drive. I was on the family's route, and we developed a friendly relationship. They'd ask how the recent rains might affect the harvest, and they'd jump at a chance to be shown the field where those funny carrots were grown. These customers included politicians stumping in every town and hall in New Hampshire, who viewed my stand as a respite from the campaign trail. Thrifty mothers picking up fruit for their kids' lunchboxes during the week fell into this category, too. I grew to recognize these customers, to know what they liked, and to put aside something special for their weekly visits.

The next type was the bargain hunter, like the two elderly ladies on limited income who knew what I knew— that my misshapen or slightly discolored produce was fresh, clean, and great for canning, salads, soups, and pies. They prided themselves on being shrewd enough to have spotted such a deal. They came because my produce was less expensive than what they could buy in the store, and they were happiest if I could give them an even better deal once they arrived. For these customers, I always had a "bargain basket" under the table. They were happy to scoop up the lower-priced carrots that were a few days older or tomatoes too soft for slicing but perfect for sauces and soups.

I also noticed that at holiday times, or even when I put

a sign out saying "Remember Mother's Day," a fourth type of customer would appear. These folks might not show up at other times, but they were drawn in when I made special signs. Soon I had created a special area for promotions, celebrating every holiday as well as midsummer, harvest time, and back to school. Special occasions included Halloween, Thanksgiving, Easter, and the promotion of "fresh picked today."

Over time, I made a game of guessing which type of customer might show up next. After about six months of weekends and two seasons spent learning to recognize customers and what seemed to attract them, I had created a section of my stand for bargain hunters and a section for special promotions. I also set aside bags of special items for the regular customers with whom I had developed relationships. I printed my grandma's recipes for soup and casseroles, using the "green-purple-red tomatoes" I had for sale. If I had a relationship with a customer, I'd say, "I have a new recipe for you!" While waiting for customers to show up, I'd get out my crayons and draw on paper sacks—a smiling sunshine, a flower, or grass to illustrate freshness. So instead of getting just a couple of pieces of fruit, my customers would go home with a piece of my artwork. Soon, this helped me develop relationships with nearly all of my customers.

I may not have been aware of it at the time, but in order to create receptivity on the part of everyone who approached my stand, I had created ways to satisfy four distinct categories of customers.

Setting up for business at the Happiness Patch meant understanding different types of people and their differing

> ### ⤳ LESSON 3 ⤳
>
> To create receptivity with the greatest number of people, be prepared to do business in a way that makes them comfortable.

needs. Once I understood who my customers were as buying types, I was able to create a positive experience for each, to develop more relationships, and to make more sales.

Over time in the adult world of business, I began to observe that the same four basic types of customers that showed up at the Happiness Patch kept showing up, whether I was selling antiques or magazine ads, executive search services, consulting services, or professional training. When I talked to Sales Athletes, I learned that these were the same people they prepared for when approaching new clients, setting up shop, or floating a new idea. Of course, people are different, but as consumers and listeners being approached with something new, they generally fall into one of four categories.

The Four Universal Types of Customers

Quick and Easy

This buyer wants to buy quickly, painlessly, probably just once, and never again—not to make a personal connection or develop a business relationship. This type of customer stopped for a stretch, flipped me a quarter for a dime's worth of vegetables, then hopped back into his car before I could say, "Thanks!"

The quick and easy buyers are easy to spot. They may be obviously in a hurry or distracted. If you get a curt response or no response at all to your greeting, chances are the person you're dealing with simply wants a quick and easy transaction.

It can feel uncomfortable to have someone conduct a purchase, gather your informational materials, or sign a contract while they are checking their e-mail or talking to someone else on their cell phone. If people are clearly distracted by time pres-

Quick and Easy Customer

sures, children, or other tasks and just want you to handle a transaction quickly in the meantime, don't take it personally, and don't overthink the transaction. What these people value is easy, painless completion of the sale or business transaction. They don't have the time or the inclination to develop a relationship with you or to learn more about your product, service, or idea. But you can give them a satisfying experience by quietly letting them be lost in their own world while you help them take care of business. You've made the transaction just the same, effortlessly and painlessly on your part; and that's not a bad thing!

Remember that sometimes people are just too over-extended to connect with you while doing business. By making the transaction as smooth and easy as possible by respecting their state of mind (not scowling at them for being on the cell phone, not insisting they have a conversation when they're clearly lost in thought), you're more likely to see them return in a less distracted or harried frame of mind. Some people behave rudely in this way while doing business because it gives them a sense of power, but often it is just a function of too many demands at the same time.

I myself have been guilty of walking into a store while on the cell phone with an important client and silently purchasing an item by simply pointing my finger, smiling, handing the salesperson my credit card, signing the charge slip, motioning to please wrap it, taking the wrapped purchase, and then nodding goodbye—an entire transaction completed without exchanging a word. That's not the ideal way of doing business, I know, and I would never do that on a regular basis. But it was a day of intense deadline pressure for the client, and on the same day I learned that a dear friend had just suffered a heartbreaking personal setback. I wanted to send her a token of my concern but couldn't drop everything to go shopping. While taking my client's call on the way to my car, I saw in a store window just the thing I needed: a little silver heart bracelet. I pointed to the bracelet and handed over my credit card to the salesman, who ran the card, wrapped the bracelet, and handed it over in a little bag. The salesman made the transaction as simple as possible, smiling at the humor of my multitasking, and for that I was grateful. If

I am in the neighborhood again, I'll remember his shop as an easy, positive place to do business.

Providing value to a quick and easy, purely transactional customer or listener means giving them their space to be in and out of the sale quickly, without connecting on a personal level. Don't expect more, but if you make things quick and easy, they're more likely to come back in a less distracted frame of mind.

Bargain Hunter

These customers are satisfied only if they believe they've gotten the best deal at a lower price than most people are paying. This buying style holds true if they are the elderly ladies buying vegetables at the Happiness Patch; the wife of the retired general who, despite her wealth, refuses to shop anywhere but the mili-tary PX; or the corporate buyer who spends thousands of dollars on pens but won't upgrade beyond the least expensive ballpoint. To provide value to the bargain hunter, you must have options available that cost less than you would normally charge. You can offer less cost for less service or less cost for less quality, but there must be a less expensive option available to give that sense of satisfaction and value to the bargain hunter.

Bargain Hunter

Some high-end businesses refuse to put their prestigious products on sale, and many people who provide services have a set price from which they won't budge. But even these businesses recognize that significant profits can be earned when they find a way to serve the bargain hunter. Have you ever seen a marked-down or slightly chipped table at Cartier? Of course not. But even people who are bargain hunters by nature can go into Cartier and buy a leather business card holder or a fountain pen, getting the satisfaction of the prestigious name without spending what precious-jewelry clients do for the same feeling.

If you are offering services, you can package them in ways to offer something for the bargain hunter. FedEx, for example, charges less for delivering in the afternoon or in two days, instead of overnight.

A productivity consultant specializes in customized training at law firms but will do a one-hour, lower-cost packaged presentation for those who balk at the cost of training tailored to the firm. You may find that offering something for the bargain hunters gives them the comfort they need to buy more services or the expanded package down the line. Bargain hunters are out there, and they're not going to be receptive unless you have something to offer that provides them the value of feeling like they've found a bargain.

A bargain hunter may be on a limited budget, or he or she may get ego satisfaction in getting something for less than it's worth. We've all met this person. You go into his or her house and admire an appliance or a piece of furniture, and the person's immediate response is, "Ah! I got that on eBay for *half* the cost at any major department store, *new*!"

It can be painful to have someone ask you for what you have to offer for less than you believe it's worth. You might want to say, "Get out of here!" but, instead, recognize that it takes all kinds. Don't let the bargain hunter turn you off. Be prepared for this type with a lower-priced option that leaves you feeling whole and leaves them satisfied they've gotten a bargain. Each transaction needs to be seen separately and each type appreciated for what they are—customers.

Program Lovers

People like programs. The program person gets satisfaction from regular, repeat service and club membership or programs that send regular offers, discounts, and re-

Promotional Customer

minders: airline mileage programs; hotel clubs; "Buy Ten, Get One Free" lunches; the "Club Rub" ten-massage package; Wine-of-the-Month; sign up for three sessions and get the first one-hour session at half-price; buy on-line and give us your e-mail address, and you'll be on our "secret sale" list.

The possibilities for satisfying the program person are nearly endless. Whatever the value of your product, service, or idea, program people find it more valuable if you present it to them as part of a program.

People value programs because programs offer them the ability to project the cost and the profit of a product or service over time. They can gauge whether, over the period of a program, they will benefit enough from what is offered to make signing up worthwhile. Programs offer people a way to feel connected and loyal to a product or service, to be reminded about regular maintenance, and to be part of a club that provides goodies on a regular basis.

Relationship

The client, customer, or listener who wants a relationship is to be treasured. Over time, providing value to people in the way they perceive value helps you turn bargain hunters, program lovers, and even some transactional clients into relationships.

A potential relationship client is open to conversation, asks questions that build a deeper understanding of your business, and is genuinely interested in figuring out if what you are presenting offers something of value. Engage in that relationship; move it forward toward consensus on your product, service, or idea; and let the

Relationship Customer

customer or client know how much you value the experience of doing business.

Work to build relationships at every opportunity, by being responsive to questions, offering helpful information, and actively seeking ways to alleviate any concerns a prospective client or customer might have (see in Chapter 7, Eight "Something Extra" Ideas). Not all client prospects will become relationships, but if you never disappoint and consistently prove you are there to hold up your end, more of your business contacts will move into this priceless category.

Building Loyalty with Every Sale

Building and maintaining relationships is the key to your career satisfaction and security, as we'll discuss further in Part Three. Don't underestimate the importance of treating your clients well and treasuring those relationships as they grow.

- Nurture your business relationships by treating them like a member of your corporate family.
- Include them in decision making where possible, and give them early notice of new products, programs, sales, or services.
- Your relationship clients like to participate and to be heard and appreciated. If you decide to do something new and interesting, call on your relationship clients and ask their opinion of this confidential new idea.

- When you've been doing business together for a long time and understand how your businesses work and where the problems and opportunities lie, consider showing your appreciation by finding ways to become strategic partners in ventures where you can both prosper.

As you're moving through business opportunities, you may find a relationship client behaving like a bargain hunter, when in fact he or she is just testing the relationship to make sure the friendship isn't being abused. This client may ask for a discount, as in, "Don't I get the friendly Dave's discount?" Or the client may test you in other ways to make certain the relationship is not being taken for granted. Be sure to give the relationship client first notice of any discounts or bonuses. Assure those clients that they are indeed valued for more than their transactions and that they both deserve to be and will always be treated accordingly.

When you have a product, a service, or an idea you know is valuable to others, be resourceful enough to present that product, service, or idea in a way that will provide value to all four types of people. Being prepared for all types will help you create receptivity wherever you go. You'll find that providing value *in the way that others perceive value* helps you turn more of your business contacts into satisfying, long-term relationships, and those relationships will provide *you* value throughout your career.

Part Two

Turning Cold Calls into Warm Relationships

LESSON 4: To overcome fear of rejection, learn how to recognize and to communicate with six types of prospects.

LESSON 5: A good presentation adds credibility and value to anything you have to offer, including yourself.

LESSON 6: Stories have the power to break down walls to and to open doors to receptivity.

Chapter 4

Communicating with All the People, All the Time

I learned at the Happiness Patch to use speed bumps to slow down the traffic, and customers who had some interest in my produce stopped and got out of their cars. When my funny-looking fruits and vegetables were met with skepticism, I was quick to point out that it was fresher than most produce sold in the store, to show the fields where it was grown, and to offer a family recipe using the same type of vegetables.

Occasionally, a customer would show up, seem interested, pick over the fruit and look at the vegetables, then not be able to make up her mind over something as simple as whether to buy a tomato. She'd say something like, "Hmmm, this is a good buy on these tomatoes, and they are firm . . . but maybe I'll come back next week?" My response would be, "Well, tomato season is just about over, so why don't I just put a couple of these in a bag for you to take home today?"

I grew to value those customers who trusted me enough to tell me what they needed and wanted. Whether it was bargains or a recipe for using my produce, I could give it to them and they'd be more likely to return and become relationship customers.

As I learned ways to communicate with all these customers, a few drivers would whisk by my speed bumps and continue past my stand without a nod; even worse, they would roll their eyes and honk at any car slowing to pull over my way. I was just as happy these people didn't stop!

Years later, however, I met many people with the same rude attitude. When I hit Madison Avenue and began to sell advertising, people weren't driving down the road but were tucked away in their luxury offices with big windows and power views. They had assistants who held at bay anyone who approached. And, not knowing what type of person sat behind my prospective client's executive desk, often I feared the worst—a rude crabapple who would dish out harsh and total rejection.

Not only did I need speed bumps to make initial contact possible, I needed verbal strategies for communicating once I reached those potential clients. Some prospects were rude, but most were indifferent. Some were skeptical, interested, indefinite, or offered their honest objections and told me exactly where they stood. Clearly, the same approach was not going to work in every situation.

The greatest challenge was moving past my own fear of rejection in order to open the lines of communication and create receptivity to my story. Whether you're selling a product, a service, or an idea, it's natural to be a bit of a weenie when faced with the prospect of rejection; most people—even many experienced salespeople—try to avoid situations where they might be brushed aside or treated with contempt. Sadly, though, this fear can keep you from putting your solid ideas forward, limit you in your career, or cause you to settle for less than you can achieve or earn.

The driving force of my life—the need to connect—required me to reach out to complete strangers hidden behind icy skyscraper exteriors. I wanted more than anything to break through any barriers that might restrict my being able to tell the story about the product, service, or idea I truly believed was in their best interest. If I was wrong and what I had to sell was not a fit, I wanted to develop a relationship that would help me figure out why.

After a few bruising experiences with rejection and many attempts to create openings in seemingly hopeless situations, I began to break down the process of communicating with prospective buyers by viewing it as a challenging game. I found that whenever I approached someone new, that person would respond to me in one of six different ways. Once I was able to create approaches that would break through and create receptivity in each case, I became able to approach all of the people all of the time, confident I could serve even the meanest, hardest people in business. I was no longer a fearful weenie; I was a Sales Athlete.

ᕫ LESSON 4 ᕬ

To overcome fear of rejection, learn how to recognize and to communicate with six types of prospects.

Six Possible Responses to Your Approach

The six characteristic responses (verbal or implied) you'll find whenever you approach anyone new with a product, a service, or an idea are:

1. Rude
2. Indifferent
3. Skeptical
4. Interested
5. Indefinite
6. Objector

Responding to these different attitudes obviously requires different approaches. The challenge is to know to whom you are speaking, and to quickly assess which strategy will move your listener into a position of trusting you enough to tell you exactly what they need and want from the connection. You need to first identify the type of person you're dealing with and then apply the appropriate principles for creating receptivity with that type of person. Remember, this strategy only works when you are prepared with the research you need to maintain credibility with your listener once you have established an open dialogue.

The goal is to create trust and to open a dialogue in which all types of listeners will be comfortable enough to truthfully tell you any objections or concerns they might have about your product, service, or idea. Once they have made their concerns clear, you will be able to provide solutions and in doing so create bonds that will cement a positive business relationship. Here are the guidelines for reaching that goal with each type of listener you may encounter.

Rude: Don't Take It Personally

Whenever I meet a crabapple—someone who doesn't appreciate my passion to solve a problem, provide a solution, make a positive contribution, and make their life easier in some way—I want that client even more! Rude people are the most feared of all, but when you have learned how to communicate with them, you'll find they are also the most loyal. Because they won't stop to listen to new information, they frequently remain uninformed about available improvements. Once you win them over as a preferred and valued resource, rude prospects become your most loyal clients. These clients will not hesitate to tell you what they need to keep them loyal. They frequently take great pride in the decision to do business with you and to fend off your competitors.

Rude

When facing a difficult potential customer like this, remember that he or she didn't save that behavior or create it just for you. It is a tactic used regularly as a business method to shoo people away. Rude prospects believe their behavior works because it does succeed in creating a distance between themselves and any perceived outside nonsense.

Once you recognize that rude behavior is not directed at you personally, you can embrace the challenge of separating yourself in the eyes of rude people from all the other people who have disappointed them. You feel their pain, you care, and you're not going to let their growling send you away, as it might less committed competitors.

"Put me down in your calendar for June 23," one snarling prospect told me over the phone. "And when you call, I'll be sure not to be here!"

I replied with a lilt in my voice, "Ouch! What on earth has happened to you to cause you to respond with such *anger* to my wanting to drive business to your company?"

With that, I heard him loosely cover the mouthpiece of his telephone and shout to his secretary, "She got me!"

At other times, when a rude prospect comes snarling my way, I might smile, shake my head, and quietly return the volley: "That is exactly why I called! This is not a normal reaction to a call from me. You must have had a terrible experience. Tell me about it."

I call it "Going to Mount Vent." I am happy to be their sounding board as they blow off steam about how they've been ripped off, how all salespeople are conniving, how they're not about to let *me* try and con them into something they can well do without. I prefer to encourage them to vent their frustrations. When they are through, they usually feel a little silly. Not only were you listening, they were listening to themselves, too, so now most often they are willing to listen to what I have to say.

I let these prospects know that I, too, am angry with "those people" in the past who have let them down. It is people like that who are preventing my prospect from listening to the tried-and-true advantages of my services.

Indifferent: Differentiate Yourself

Throughout every aspect of your life, you are going to find people who just don't see the value of spending time with you. Indifference is the most common response you're likely to encounter. This person may not be overtly rude, but he or she is absolutely confident you have nothing of value to offer and therefore sees no reason for spending time with you. There are a variety of ways to communicate indifference: "Thank you, but I'm satisfied with my existing resource." Or "Oh, we don't need those, we don't have any use for that." Underlying such statements or an attitude of indifference is the unspoken message, "People are always trying to sell me something I don't need, and I don't want to waste my time."

You may recognize this as the buyer for whom I had to install speed bumps along the road. To slow down people who are up to their neck in details or overwhelmed in a deal-a-minute world, the strategy is to put in place speed bumps that help you differentiate yourself from the hordes of messages and mediocrity besieging these potential clients every hour of every day.

Your job with indifferent prospects is to differentiate yourself from all those people who have wasted their time and to present yourself as a knowledgeable professional who will increase their profits each and every time you connect.

Indifferent

Your opening strategy is to produce four or five speed bumps from your checklist of ways to first introduce yourself; phone, voice mail, assistant, e-mail, fax, traditional letter, networking.

You have a story to tell. Mine is always the same. I promise to make the experience as easy, positive, and informative as possible. Please note there is no single way; your selection of speed bumps depends on whom you are trying to reach.

Speed Bump Example:

1. Call and connect with the assistant and ask for guidance. Ask if he or she would be kind enough to pop you into voice mail.
2. Produce a short and to-the-point letter. Letters still work and differentiate you from the e-mail clutter.

3. Make a follow-up phone call. Ask the assistant if you can e-mail, and then CC the assistant.
4. E-mail the client with the same message that you left with the assistant when you first called, reiterated in the letter, voice mail, and now e-mail.
5. The fifth approach is equal to my last sign on the route: "Happiness Is Just Around the Corner." I offer the opportunity to provide, in a short meeting, a strong return on the person's time invested.

At The Sales Athlete, Inc., my message is always clear: "If you would like to improve sales and profits, you may want to consider hiring a Sales Athlete. In just a few minutes, I can show you how to trade your weakest link for a high-performance Sales Athlete." I believe it, and I mean it.

Skeptical: Three Undeniable Facts

I firmly believe that if there is a skepticism you cannot answer with three undeniable facts, you allow that skepticism to block you, and therefore you do not believe or have the confidence you need to tell your story. For this reason, you need a Skeptic Emergency Kit.

Skeptical people believe they have good reasons to distrust you and whatever it is you represent. A skeptic does not believe a word of what you are saying, so it's very easy to become defensive or to respond emotionally. When someone questions your ethics or accuses you of not valuing the truth, it is bound to hurt. Don't get mad; get ready to present your facts.

Recognize that the skeptic has reason to distrust. The last person who tried to win his support turned out to be a phony. The office copier doesn't work, and nobody answers the repair number. The car he just bought turned out to be a lemon.

Skeptical

What you need when dealing with skeptics are three absolute truths—indisputable, credible facts—that will overcome the belief that you are trying to take their money and give less than fair value in return. Your briefcase should contain a "Skeptic Emergency Kit": as much proof as you can gather from three reliable sources that your product, service, or idea has been tested, is of value, and has been enjoyed and pronounced by others to be the finest quality. Not six or seven facts—wouldn't that look defensive?—just three: for example, testimonials, research data, and your guarantee.

You might include articles from industry or general business magazines showing your product to be on the leading edge of its field, or testimonials from front-runners in the skeptic's business who have found success with your company. If you are presenting an idea to a skeptical decision maker, you might present evidence of how your company has saved money, increased sales and profits, or improved productivity at other firms; research data from a reliable source about the importance of solving the problem addressed by your idea; and your company's guarantee.

By not looking, acting, or talking like a typical salesperson, you can actually create credibility. By offering three indisputable facts—each selected as proof that your idea is valuable—you can remove skepticism and win trust.

Important tip about presenting your three indisputable facts: When you present them, stack them on top of each other, and then break them down one by one. For example, the prospect responds, "Everyone says the same thing. How do I know this works?" You would answer, "This is a very good question. Let me show you (1) XYZ data, (2) quotes from happy clients and business leaders just like yourself who are doing business with us, and (3) our 'Satisfaction Guarantee.'" And then present each one separately, giving your client-to-be the opportunity to review each and to ask questions.

Interested: Don't Forget to Tell Your Story

Compared to the rude, indifferent, or skeptical, the interested person must seem like a gift from heaven. "I'm so glad you called. Today's a perfect day. When can you come in?" Isn't this the ideal call? Maybe not. When you hear words like that, be grateful, but beware. Sometimes people are so interested at the outset that they don't give you an opportunity to let them know the best way to take advantage of what you have to offer. For instance, this person may ask, "How much does this cost?" without understanding the true value and benefit of doing business with your company.

Just to be safe, you would respond, "I would be happy to give you the price, but there are so many ways to buy. May I ask what made you decide to see me today?" The prospect might say, "I was at the Rotary Club today, and I was told by a fellow Rotarian of the success they had doing business with you." Your response: "Great! Let me ask you a few questions and see what we can do for you, so you enjoy the same easy and positive experience."

Never take interested prospects for granted. Find out specifically what interested them in the first place, so that you'll better understand their needs and be able to address them one by one.

Be prepared to meet all objections and to pin down details. Why? Because their initial interest may have been sparked by a fantasy that you will deliver something you may not in fact be able to deliver.

Interested

Over time and with a commitment to excellence, I

have been fortunate enough to build a strong and valuable word-of-mouth referral network. The phone will ring, and someone on the other end of the line will say, "I need a Sales Athlete." You certainly would agree this is a fortunate moment—an interested client. My response is always the same: "Who referred you, and what did they tell you?"

"I was told that The Sales Athlete, Inc., hung the moon and took their company to number one in the business."

At that point, I need to explain, "This client hired three experienced Sales Athletes and has added one or two over the past three years. I also understand that over that time the company has taken over the premier position in its market." In other words, it takes more than a phone call to reach that level of success.

Without qualifying this interested prospect, her expectations would have been unreal, and possibly the transaction would have been less than satisfactory for the caller as well as for the Sales Athlete placed in the position with unreal expectations.

Indefinite: Lead the Way

An indefinite prospect is more likely to create exasperation than fear. His customary response is to delay because of timing, or to claim that someone else must help make the decision, or to give any other explanation that leads you to believe he is a prospective client, but that it is just a matter of how and when.

When you are delayed, the reasons are simple: The

prospect needs more information, doesn't have the power to make the decision, or is delaying a decision in order to lower your expectations. Finally, he or she may be too nice to just say, "No."

When you call, the indefinite prospect might say, "Call me next February," or "My partner makes this decision," or "The budgets are all spent."

Your job is to determine what you need to do *today* to determine how you can best serve this client. Let him know you will make a note to call in February and ask, "If I were looking out for your best interests between now and next February, what would you suggest I look for on your behalf?" When the prospect says something like, "Look for deep discounts," you'll know the real objection is the price of your product, service, or idea.

Indefinite

Don't wait until next February to let the indefinite prospect know there are many ways to buy. Explain that in just a few minutes, you can show him or her how to best meet the stated objective.

When you are told that a partner makes this decision, simply ask for the partner's name. Then add, "With what you know about our company and what you know about how your partner makes this kind of decision, what would you suggest I include in my presentation?" This approach, too, will draw out any objections, enabling you to meet what the prospective client needs.

"Include your guarantees and lots of research," the indefinite person may say. "He is very skeptical. He has been ripped off before." Now you know you need to present your Skeptic Emergency Kit.

Some indefinite customers are simply uncomfortable saying "No." Try to mentally place this client side by side with you by relating a story: "Our happiest clients started out just like you. Let's take a look at how they use our company and how we became their most valued resource."

As my grandmother trained me, "You never push a noodle, you pull a noodle." Don't give the indefinite person two choices. Lead him or her instead.

"I hear you," you respond to the balky indecision. "I am asking for a few minutes of your time, and I strongly believe it is overwhelmingly in your best interest to invest a few minutes with me to lay out my idea. Will you please look at your calendar? Does Tuesday between 10 and 10:15 A.M. work for you?"

Objector: Straightforward and Honest

The objector is the best possible type of client because he or she trusts you enough to tell you exactly what you need to do to make it happen. These open communicators know what is important. They want to find the best resources to help build their businesses, and they know how to ask for

what they want and need. If you have what they have
asked for, you are in.

If you review the advice
I have given for all the prospect types, you can see that
the overall strategy is to turn
whatever type of prospect you
face—rude, skeptical, indifferent, indefinite, or even interested—into someone who
trusts you enough to become
an objector: to tell you what
he or she honestly needs and
wants from you.

Objector

When faced with any of the six possible responses,
the Sales Athlete works to create an open, clear dialogue
that brings the best results to all parties. Can you think of
a better way to pin down details than to be given a clear
statement of why an idea doesn't work and under which
circumstances it would?

Once you have gathered all the facts you need to meet
every objection, you will be able to drive solutions and to
create strong and dynamically loyal relationships throughout your life. The approach with skeptics should be to
earn their trust so they will trust you enough to openly tell
you their objections. You want rude people to focus on
their real objections, not simply on objecting to your exis-
tence. You want indifferent people to listen and to then
offer you their objections. As long as you are dealing with
objectors and you can answer their objections, there is a

The Golden Apple

bona fide opportunity to turn those prospects into satisfied customers. Objectors trust that you have the ability to solve their problems. They will openly outline what they believe are their problems and what they need from you to solve these problems.

It's unwise to sell something to a person who genuinely does not want or need your product, service, or idea. It *is* wise—and critical to your success—to know how to determine, through rapport-building information gathering, how much of a listener's resistance is based on hidden emotional factors rather than on objections that can be satisfied. Regardless of your audience, it is also important that you know how to add value to your message with the way you present your ideas and *yourself.*

Chapter 5

The Well-Polished Presenter

Because I was still in elementary school, my business at the Happiness Patch was limited to weekends, summers, and vacations. Every morning at the stand started early. I'd get up, place my signs, haul boxes of my bumpy vegetables to the wooden spool table, and then begin waiting for customers. Since I had no idea who those customers might be, and most likely they'd be strangers, I dressed for these potential customers in the same way as I would for the "company" my parents would invite over on rare occasion. Of course, I didn't put on a special church outfit, but instead of wearing old shorts in the summer and coveralls in the winter, I tried to look nice in my best sweater and slacks and to have my hair combed and clean.

Once at the stand, I was always careful to use my "company" manners: greeting people in a friendly way; looking them in the eye rather than shyly at my feet; asking polite and interested questions such as, "Has the drive been pretty this afternoon, ma'am?"; and always, always, saying, "Thank you. Please come again." It was important, I knew, to present oneself as politely as possible when meeting strangers, and no strangers were more important than those special customers who would stop their fancy cars just to come to my stand.

By the second weekend, I thought I was all set. Signs were placed, vegetables were on the table, and I was waiting in clean clothes, smiling politely. But when the first customers came, they'd open the conversation by asking, "What've you got here?" Or, "The sign said you had cucumbers . . . ?" And they'd peer into my boxes of vegetables to see what was inside. Fortunately, in fairly short order, Miss August, the teacher who kindly helped me make my signs, stopped by to offer another gentle suggestion.

"Kathy," she said, "I think you need to work on your display."

It was a kind suggestion because, in fact, I didn't have a display. I simply had boxes of vegetables, some of them jumbled together. It was not the most attractive way to present vegetables that, lumpy and misshapen as they were, could certainly benefit from some careful arrangement.

What's more, when my first customers picked from the boxes a bunch of grapes or a couple of tomatoes, I realized they had nowhere to *put* their purchases, unless they'd brought their own bags. Packaging of some kind would help, too.

The next day, I added two more steps to my process of preparing to serve customers. I arranged my vegetables by type and size, trying to mix colors in attractive ways. I made sure they were clean and shiny, and I always put the most attractive pieces in front.

I also brought with me to the stand a stack of used but clean and neatly folded grocery bags. To while away the time between customers, I also brought crayons. On each bag I drew a picture—a smiling, shining sun; a bright red tomato; a grapevine; little green shoots popping up from the brown earth on a spring day.

It didn't take long for me to realize customers were more likely to look at everything I had when my produce was displayed more attractively. I was also amazed to find that when customers had a paper bag to put things in, they bought more! And when the paper bag was hand decorated by the budding artist standing before them, more often than not, they put a couple more pieces of produce into their bags. The effort I put into presenting and packaging actually enhanced the value of the produce inside and encouraged customers to buy more.

> ⇜ **LESSON 5** ⇝
>
> A good presentation adds credibility and value to anything you have to offer, including yourself.

The lessons I learned about packaging and presentation are true today for every one of the Sales Athletes I represent and the clients I advise. They apply to the products you may sell; the way you present your ideas; and, every bit as important, the way you present yourself, twenty-four hours a day.

A crayon-decorated grocery sack may be a far cry from a Tiffany box wrapped in a perfectly tied silken ribbon, but both packages tell the same story: When the package is crisp, what's inside seems more special. Extra effort put into packaging and presentation lends credibility to what's being presented.

Now, imagine walking into Tiffany to buy something special in that exquisite signature box and being greeted by a salesperson dressed in jeans cut low enough to expose her navel ring, tapping the register with three-inch, glittered nails, and chewing gum while saying, "May I help you?" Preposterous image, isn't it? You know it's preposterous because people who work at Tiffany know they must convey the elegance of the products they are selling. Likewise, you won't win receptivity to your products, services, ideas, or candidacy unless you reflect positively on the idea or product you are presenting.

The 24-Hour Professional

Being a professional 24/7 doesn't mean that to succeed in your career you should become a workaholic with no life. As a professional, how you present yourself matters not just from nine to five, Monday through Friday, when you're certain to be with coworkers or clients. It matters when you're out in the community, on the road, at the grocery store, or at a restaurant. At any time, you may meet or be seen by a business associate or someone who is potentially a client, customer, or employer. Your credibility will be judged on social occasions and at times when you least expect to be seen, not only during normal business hours.

Dress

Before anyone sits down to hear you present a product or proposal, he or she has formed an impression of you. Yes, we'd like to think that "dress for success" is a vestige of the past and that a good work product should move us past our physical appearance. The truth is, however, the clothes you choose send a signal about your judgment, your willingness to stay current, your taste, and your sense of style. All of these things play a role in how effective you are in creating receptivity and conveying credibility.

Effort put into the sharpest presentation materials for your proposal or idea will be wasted if your listener becomes fixated on your inappropriately short skirt or clashing, outdated necktie.

Nothing you wear, say, or project should restrict receptivity to what you are presenting.

I am frequently approached for career coaching by people who are smart and good at the work they do and are therefore confused about why they're having such trouble getting past the first job interview or why they keep getting passed over for promotions. Often the answer is staring at them in the mirror, but they fail to see it and nobody has been kind or courageous enough to point it out. Consider the woman who aspires to meet customers and get out of the back office, but who dresses twenty years too young, in clothing too tight, with shoes too extreme and badly colored hair out of style. Or the man with dirty fingernails and with clunky brown shoes shouting from under a blue pinstriped suit.

Even if fashion is not your thing, if you have any lack of confidence in this area, it pays to do your own makeover. Pick up a fashion magazine regularly or seek the help of a seasoned, qualified fashion consultant—not to spend a fortune on whatever's trendy, but to find out which looks are flattering and which are not for your body type, age, and work culture.

One stifling day last summer, we had a client in The Sales Athlete, Inc., office interviewing candidates for a wonderful West Coast management position. Right out of the box, he passed on a candidate because she was wearing no slip and her dress was transparent. Lately, I hear employers complain about executive men in golf shirts and women slipping into the bare shoulder, midriff-peeking look. And, yes, visible tummies and visible tattoos do limit career opportunities.

In the sweltering summer months, it's sometimes tempting to let go of propriety and ditch the stockings or tie. In business, however, there's decorum year-round. So I repeat this one simple rule: Is there anything about your selection of dress that would diminish the power of the message you are about to deliver? If the answer is even possibly "maybe," it's best to err on the side of propriety.

To make it easier for all of us to answer that question, I'd like to begin a movement to end Casual Fridays. This practice began at a time when employers couldn't afford pay raises and were looking for ways to improve morale. It has resulted in some people dressing in belly-baring clothes and in workout pants for 20 percent of every workweek—on the day before the weekend when, often, the most important business deals are sealed. That's why, at The Sales Athlete, Inc., we don't have Casual Friday.

What happens if an important potential client comes into the office or a major client calls an emergency meeting across town? If a prospective employer calls asking to see you on Friday, are you going to say, "Gee, I'd love to see you about the job of my dreams, but I'm having a Casual Friday. So I hope you don't mind that I'm wearing a gym suit." A successful person is prepared to do business every day.

Social Skills

It's hard to have credibility when you're chasing a sausage off the edge of a table or if you've got something hanging on your chin as if by magic. Table manners—everything from where to leave your napkin to how you chew your food—can signal the kiss of death to a potential client or employer; or manners can seal a deal because of the credibility and taste you convey while sharing a business meal.

We are rarely, rarely told of our transgressions. But talk with your mouth full or make a lesser faux pas, and your guest will go away thinking, "Piggy!"

Business entertainment can be a minefield if you don't have the confidence and good judgment that come with training and practice. One of my clients once made the business meal mistake of ordering hard sausage at a lunch where she expected to be given a final offer on a job she'd coveted for more than a year. Right at the point of salary negotiation, she speared her sausage, which jumped off the plate and into the employer's lap! After the incident, the interviewer decided not to hire her because she "wasn't polished enough." Fortunately, I persuaded the client to change his mind. The candidate learned forever the lesson of not ordering difficult or tricky-to-eat items while doing business.

I've had major employers call me seeking to fill top positions that people within their own companies are perfectly qualified to fill. When I probe as to why they are looking outside the firm, as often as not the reason is that the person in-house is fine at doing the work but doesn't "present well." In one case, a manager ruled out considering an existing employee for a big promotion simply because when he took her to lunch to discuss his plans for her future, she picked up a steak knife and sliced her bread lengthwise, instead of tearing a small piece off with her hand. It seems like a trivial thing, but it was enough for this manager to determine that his employee lacked the sophistication necessary for the job he had in mind.

Manners are a difficult subject because all of us want to believe we were brought up right. Sadly, however, social graces at mealtime are becoming a lost art, as busy families scatter and eat on the run. If table manners were a casualty of your busy childhood, it's now your job to train yourself in this important indicator of social credibility.

If you have any hesitation about etiquette at meals, brush up with Tiffany & Co.'s little blue book, *Table Manners for Teenagers*. Search the Web, and read Miss Manners until you have every confidence you can negotiate any mealtime meeting with grace. Take a refined colleague to lunch, and ask him or her to honestly and critically observe your behavior.

In "Business Entertaining," one of the most popular classes I've taught at The Sales Athlete, Inc., I teach trainees how to count the bites required to complete a meal. Knowing how long it takes to finish an entrée is important, because you want to pace the meal in a way that makes your guest comfortable. Imagine that the client is going to order the chopped chef's salad, for example. That's more than one hundred bites—a salad, but a big meal and time-consuming to eat. Suppose you want to order the scampi, which is four shrimp. On the surface, this doesn't look like a bad order, but unless you're planning on doing most of the talking at the meal, your plate will be taken quickly unless you are willing to continually shoo away the busboy, leaving your client feeling rushed while eating alone.

Social skills for a professional go beyond the dining table, of course, and include social sensitivity and political astuteness in the workplace. If you talk down to your boss, behave rudely to your client's executive secretary, or fail to recognize and respect the hierarchy and culture of the business you are working for or with, your political cluelessness will harm your career prospects. Do your homework on the office protocols, organization chart, and social landscape of any business by which you are employed or with which you interact. Always behave politely and with respect to everyone, every time.

Just as it pays to take care with the way you dress any time you leave your home, you should never leave your best manners at the office or the dining table. Kindness toward and tolerance for others are worth cultivating not only for ethical and moral reasons, but because failure to engage in both virtues can cause you professional harm. Imagine that you're going down the road and someone stops you to ask for directions. You blow them off because you're going to an important meeting, and then it turns out that the person who asked directions is the person you're supposed to meet!

A man I'll call Wayne came into my service one day, and we were very high on him, intending to submit his resume to a client for a terrific career opportunity. That same day, I was in the car with that client on our way to lunch. My client, talking while driving, pulled into another lane, failing to notice that at the same time, another car was trying to merge in from the other side. It turned out the other driver was Wayne, who didn't see me but honked and yelled at my client, "*&*@% you!*" I knew immediately I couldn't place Wayne in this Sales Athlete position because of the way he allowed himself to publicly lose control. I called Wayne, let him know what had happened, and reminded him of our "your next employer is watching" adage.

Your next employer is watching. Your neighbors are coming to conclusions. It's a small world.

If all this is making you too self-conscious to venture outside of your house, please remember that style, social graces, and the confidence they bring are really not that complicated. They just require attention and practice.

My friend Phillip Slagter, a superb artist, tells a lovely parable about a field of yams. In every field of sweet yams, he says, there is at least one nasty, bitter one. And when the yams are all harvested and mashed together into holiday pies, we all get a bit of that nasty yam inside of us. So remember, if you do commit a social faux pas, apologize quickly and move on, vowing to pay better attention in the future. And when someone is rude or careless with you, don't take it personally and don't lash back. Just recognize that the person's nasty yam is popping out, and let it go.

Beyond Manners—Attitude

Of the thousands of corporate client requests for executive communicators that I have received, I have never received one that said, "Send me all the bitter, put-upon, hostile, and sarcastic ones—the ones who are tense and edgy or tired and humorless."

We are in the business of negotiating. We're executive communicators, and conflict is contrary to who we are. I cannot further the career of a difficult, inflexible person. Bad attitudes create office conflicts that direct everyone's energies into placating the difficult person rather than finding solutions that bring profit.

No amount of skill in your profession can compensate for a bad attitude. My service tackles many problems created not by a salesperson's poor production but by his or her poor attitude and style. Employers will say, "He brought in five orders this month. That's not the problem. It just isn't worth what he's doing to the rest of the company and what he's taking out of us with his pain-in-the-neck personality."

Sales Athletes don't walk around with phony grins, glad-handing everywhere they go; they genuinely feel empathy for the problems of customers and have a passion for their work that brings continued success. Most important, though, they have the social sensitivity to know that even when they're a little low on energy or enthusiasm, it pays to act as if they're not. If you've tried this, you'll know the miracle that occurs when behaving positively actually lifts your spirits and creates positive feelings.

An effective presenter also remembers that the presentation is "about the client, not about me," says Erich Linker, senior vice president of national advertising for ImpreMedia, LLC. When entering a prospective client's office, you should actively observe the environment for clues that will help you to begin the conversation. Include in your presentation remarks that reflect your desire to concern yourself with the things the client cares about. Is there baseball memorabilia everywhere? You might recall an experience at a game of the client's favorite team. Do you have kids the same age as the children in her picture frame or love the very kind of chocolate he has by the bowlful on his desk?

On very hot summer days, Linker arrives at clients' offices carrying an iced tea and an iced coffee, offers the client a choice, and takes the drink that is left. That sets the stage for his presentation with bonding in a way that's both more thoughtful and more effective than the tired, "Hot day out there!"

When following up his visit with a thank-you note, Linker might include a special piece of chocolate for the chocolate lover or a reference to some other genuinely shared or observed interest. Empathy with your client should begin from the minute you walk in the door and should be at the core of your presentation and any business relationship you develop afterward.

Packaging Counts

Once you are confident that nothing about your own appearance, attitude, or manners will cause hesitation in your listener, it's time to polish the presentation of your product, service, or idea. Whatever you are selling, yourself included, will be seen as more credible when people feel you've taken the time to organize your materials and to make sure they are sharp and up to date. A presentation should help your listener understand clearly and without effort what you are presenting.

I spent thousands of dollars on a high-end color printer, and when I'm presenting to a client, I use high-quality bond paper that is heavier, crisper, and more elegant than the workaday paper I use for draft copies. It costs more than double for this bolder, brighter, high-impact paper, but what a bargain it is for its ability to convey to my client the feeling of quality, of something extra, in what I'm proposing.

With today's computer capability, anyone can take a class for a few hours and learn to use the tools that create fantastic presentations. Move around and look at other people's presentations, and take note of techniques that would give your ideas more credibility. It doesn't matter if it is a PowerPoint with flash movies or a less glitzy presentation that is clearly and appealingly documented with spreadsheets and charts—graphic displays to underscore your key messages. There's just no excuse for not taking advantage of technology to make your presentations more credible.

Your presentation, just like your speed bumps, should create a pleasurable experience for your listener and result in a greater willingness to do business with you. Clearly, your presentation cannot bore, offend, or waste the time of your listener. Your job is to keep it crisp, engaging, substantive, and as short as possible.

Your presentation should move you toward consensus with the listener, regardless of whether the listener is initially indifferent, skeptical, interested, or indefinite or has objections to what you say. In the next chapter, you'll learn how to structure a presentation in a way that will create receptivity, even to new ideas.

Chapter 6

Storytelling Selling

When new customers arrived at the Happiness Patch expecting to see produce in familiar colors and shapes, their initial reaction was, at best, puzzled.

"This carrot's shaped like a bunny!" a child shouted.

"Do you have any tomatoes that aren't so . . . bumpy?" his mother would ask.

I had little time to turn the customer's skepticism into appreciation. The only way to succeed was by telling the story of my produce stand—a short story that would bring her into my world on the farm and convince her that a bumpy tomato straight from the farm has as much value as a perfectly shaped grocery store specimen.

"Let me tell you about these special fruits and vegetables," I'd say. "These are fresh and healthy, straight from the farm you see right here. And these carrots and tomatoes with funny shapes are exactly the kind my family eats every night. We put them in soups, stews, and side dishes. I've hand-printed some recipes we use, in fact." And I'd hand her a recipe. "They're every bit as delicious as any you'll find in the store—fresher, in fact, because I picked them myself just this morning. And the best part is that I can sell them to you for less than what you could buy the same produce for at the grocery store in town!"

In just those few words, I'd painted a picture of my

family enjoying a nutritious meal. I'd passed on a recipe that would help the customer picture her family cooking and eating the same hearty country fare as my family on the farm. She'd never imagined buying produce that looked so irregular. But by telling a story about those vegetables, by creating a picture and putting her in that picture, she was able to appreciate their value.

When I told that simple story of my family growing, setting aside, and eating the misshapen produce in delicious recipes, drawing my customers into the story by creating a picture for them, they saw me not as a salesperson but as the girl on the farm eating healthy meals with her family. They could envision themselves eating at the same table; and in that moment, they were in on the secret: My bumpy fruits and vegetables *were* as valuable as grocery store produce; they just didn't look like the ones that cost two to three times as much.

⤳ LESSON 6 ⤳

Stories have the power to break down walls and to open doors to receptivity.

At The Sales Athlete, Inc., I continue to use storytelling to create receptivity because no other executive search, career coaching, and sales training service operates the way we do. We tirelessly scour a broad cross section of networking opportunities to find the top-performing talent in executive sales and marketing, then provide training and mentoring for this talent and whatever services these Sales Athletes and our client companies need to meet their professional best. We consistently hear that our level of service is rare in the fields of executive search, training, and special assignment consultation. So when a client sought our help in filling the position of vice president for marketing strategy for a television network, we suggested a terrific talent whose most recent position was in strategic marketing at a major film studio.

The initial reaction was the equivalent of "This carrot's shaped like a bunny!" Then I described how the network and the studio assignment had a great deal in common and showed the client that all the market sectors being addressed by the network were also addressed by the studio's marketing vision for the coming year. It turned out that this talent was the perfect candidate. The same was true of a former nurse I placed in executive sales with a business products firm. Didn't the nurse have experience convincing patients to comply with the doctors' orders? Also, managing a trauma team under constant and extreme pressure was an excellent skill for moving potential customers to implement organizational change through new technology. She turned out to excel at selling postal meters to corporations, even though her potential employer couldn't see her in executive sales and thought she was like a "bunny-rabbit-shaped carrot."

Not many years after I left the farm, I myself was a novel concept—a young woman selling magazine advertisements in a field then completely dominated by men. I was launching a new product for which there had been no demographic research, no prior sales statistics that I could point to, no success stories I could share. I was confronted with the questions that face all people who are innovators or who want to spur interest in an idea or product that is different from what has come before: How do you generate receptivity to something that is brand new? How do you instill appreciation for something about which there is no common frame of reference to share with your listeners? It's important to do as much research as possible, to bring credibility to your product, service, or idea. But even when you do have numbers to help you create receptivity, your listener will be more receptive if you put faces to those numbers.

New Ideas: How to Show, Tell, and Sell

When your idea is new and you don't have numbers to prove its value, create receptivity with a story that helps your listener picture what it is you're proposing and why it is of value. I learned to do this by writing recipes and telling the story of how my family valued our bumpy vegetables and, later, by showing up at the doors of company presidents as myself: "That Cosmopolitan Girl."

At that time—the early 1970s—a typical sales call would involve a cigar-smoking man in a business suit, offering to take clients out for a two-martini lunch. Difficult as it is for today's young women to believe, help-wanted ads at that time were in many places segregated by gender, with jobs for women in business largely limited to the secretarial pool. Yes, there were retail sales jobs—jobs for which women were paid less than men and that offered little hope for career advancement. But calling on company presidents to sell a product or idea? That was not yet a woman's job. The truth was, nearly all business executives were men, and executive businessmen did not often take women, particularly young women, seriously in business.

So how was I, a twenty-something redhead in an A-line dress, pumps, and matching hat and gloves, to be taken seriously in the world of executive sales? Not only were prospective clients unaccustomed to doing business straight up with a young woman like me, but most were older than my father. I would be the first woman who would pick up the phone and ask for an appointment to come and sell them something. Adding to the challenge of being young and female, what I was selling—*Cosmopolitan* magazine—was the first of its kind. While there were well-established women's and fashion magazines, none had ever been geared to the interests of young, single women living in metropolitan areas, women who had *chosen* to delay marriage and family in favor of a career. The closest thing, I suppose, was *Playboy*; and that wasn't close at all.

There'd been no focus groups or market research to define this demographic, though clearly it existed. *Cosmo* editor in chief Helen Gurley Brown had just created news with her book, *Sex and the Single Girl*, and now was ready to launch a new magazine idea for the millions of young women living as singles in a cosmopolitan city. But the notion of women living happily as singles, let alone a concept such as today's *Sex and the City*, really hadn't penetrated the culture. Clearly, I would have to break through some barriers.

Remembering the Happiness Patch and how the story of my vegetables broke down resistance to their unusual shapes and colors, I decided to tell my prospective clients the story of me: the young woman who represented a market they may not have considered. I would create a picture that would allow them to be comfortable with me and receptive to the idea that, even as a young woman, I could greatly enhance their business.

The first part of the story was: "Hi! I'm young, I'm single, I live in New York City. And if you want to sell products to me and the thousands of young women like me, you want to advertise in *Cosmopolitan*!" Right away, by the way I looked and the way I introduced myself, I created a picture of the market these executives would reach if they were receptive to my idea. I was not unlike the scores of women these executives had seen on the subway or on the streets at lunch hour—women making their way as young professionals, trying to find balance and satisfaction in their careers and relationships. But to get these men accustomed to relating to me in their world, I needed to draw them into mine.

My stories continued to create pictures of how people like me were interested in hearing about and were willing to buy the things my prospective clients had to sell. Once I told a story that included their products in the lives of young women like me, these surprised-looking advertising executives began to believe I was the face of a market they'd been missing and should miss no more.

I went to Hanes Hosiery and told the story of how every single workday, I put on my hosiery and bought far more pairs than the suburban housewives targeted by other women's magazines. There was no research to prove this, so I went out and did my own, asking the sales clerks at Lord & Taylor who was buying their Hanes hosiery. The answer? "Working women. Housewives these days are wearing pants and not buying as many pairs as frequently as working women." I told that story and then opened up the magazine and showed how every single page featured women baring their legs in business suits and party dresses. Every one of those women was a potential Hanes customer. Then I flipped through the pages of magazines the clients were advertising in, showing photos of women in slacks, slacks, slacks, and slacks.

Because I was the most junior of all the salespeople, I was given the accounts that everyone had tried but no one could sell. These are referred to humorously in the industry as the "fleas on the tail of a dead dog" accounts, given to the new kid because it was assumed she couldn't lose what had already been deemed hopeless. One of these accounts was the office products market; the common wisdom was that selling this market in a hip new women's magazine was bound to result in rejection after rejection. Companies like IBM, Correct-a-Type correction tape, and office stationers and supply firms had never before advertised in women's magazines; so this was a third barrier to cross. I knew, however, that young women like me worked in offices and used those supplies and equipment. To tell their story, I enlisted the help of my sister, Elaine, who then was a secretary to a partner at a prominent law firm.

I went to Elaine's office with a camera and photographed her typing at her desk, looking into the camera with a big smile. I blew her picture up to an eight-by-ten;

and on the stationery of her law firm, she typed a memo to her boss:

Dear Mr. Jones,

You are a senior partner at this law firm and as your secretary, I feel it important to recommend that we acquire an IBM electric typewriter as soon as possible.

This is based on my feeling that you're too important for us to be typing up correspondence on a ten-year-old typewriter.

I bought a double picture frame. On the left side I put the memo and on the right side the photo of my sister at her desk, typing on the ten-year-old typewriter. Into my briefcase it went.

When I arrived for my first appointment with IBM, the response was quick and unequivocal. "We have no intention of advertising in a woman's magazine," the executive snapped.

I responded, "I'm sorry you feel that way because I'm here to tell you that our working readers dramatically influence the purchase of typewriters."

I took out my briefcase, opened up the double picture frame, and handed it across the executive's desk. He looked at it and then asked his secretary to bring in his sales manager, of whom he asked, "How influential do you think secretaries are in buying our typewriters?"

The sales manager responded honestly, "I always ask the secretary of a prospect company if she will try out our

IBM electric. Once she does, she is the one that gets the company to buy it."

Suddenly *Cosmopolitan*, which had page after page of ads for Revlon, Clairol, Max Factor, and other women's cosmetic products, also had four-color, two-page layouts from IBM. I went on to sell National Cash Register, their typewriting paper division, and a typing correction tape firm, all by telling these businesses the story of the office professionals who had the most influence in buying their products—young, single, professional women.

Not long afterward, I joined the launching team for the first controlled-circulation consumer magazine in America, *Girl Talk* magazine. This was a magazine distributed only to beauty salons, and it was edited for the woman sitting in a beauty salon under a hair dryer. Its business magic was in the numbers: One copy would be mailed to seventy-eight thousand beauty salons, and the question asked of potential advertisers was, "Do you believe one woman a day would pick up this magazine and read it while sitting under the dryer?" Because the answer was always positive, we could assume thirty readers per month per single copy. Therefore, we printed seventy-eight thousand copies and charged advertisers to reach two-million-plus readers.

How did we convince these advertisers? With a story—beginning with a vivid picture—of the woman who represented an untapped market.

First, I went to the hat manufacturing section of New York's garment district, where I asked a milliner to create eight-inch-high domed hats—reminiscent of hair dryers—

in several colors. I set up appointments with Sears, Maytag, and Minute Maid Orange Juice. I had absolutely no sales figures to back up my presentation because the magazine was brand new.

I began with, "Let me tell you about this new idea," and then quickly popped the hat down over my ears.

"I'm stuck under a hair dryer at a beauty salon, with only this magazine to read," I'd say, then, raising my voice to a shout, "AND I CAN'T HEAR ANYTHING! I AM A CAPTIVE READER OF YOUR ADVERTISING MESSAGE. AND I'M OUT OF THE HOUSE, MOST LIKELY PLANNING TO STOP OFF AT A STORE AND BUY YOUR PRODUCTS ON MY WAY HOME!"

I'd stand in the office of the prospective client and yell, once again, "HEY! I'M UNDER A HAIR DRYER, AND I CAN'T HEAR A THING! I AM COMPLETELY FOCUSED ON THE ONE THING I HAVE IN MY HAND TO READ!"

By creating this vivid picture, I sold five pages an issue to Sears, Colgate, Bufferin, and Minute Maid. The orange juice company even agreed they should run a holiday spread around the Fourth of July, remembering not the minutemen but the minute maids' contribution to the American Revolution.

Painting a picture of another untapped market helped me to create demand and achieve success in sales during the worst recession of my lifetime. It was 1973, a time of gasoline shortages and price spikes, with lines around the block at gas stations. Even wealthy people were pinching pennies, not purchasing many little luxuries.

It was in this environment that I sold advertising into

Women's Wear Daily's consumer sister publication, *W*, a high-fashion magazine designed to appeal to the most affluent and fashionable women in the world. To convince financially stretched advertisers to stretch themselves further for this new product, I'd have to tell a compelling, low-risk story to advertising buyers about why the readers of *W* were an important demographic for them to reach in the current down economy.

W—the Window to the World of Luxury Living, I said, would be read by two hundred thousand of the most affluent trendsetters, representing the most profitable customers of high-end and specialty retailers. We knew this because *W* had purchased the mailing lists of the crème de la crème of the finest retailers in the United States, and these lists became the charter subscribers for *W*.

These readers have their own sense of style and sit in the front rows of the most important fashion shows in the world. They are rain-or-shine customers: Regardless of the highs or lows of the economy, they remain true to the importance of fashion as the most emulated women in the world.

In those tough times of war and gas lines, my story explained, the *W* reader was an economic secret weapon for fashion designers who distributed their good through high-end and specialty stores. It worked! *W* advertising revenues thrived, despite tough times.

By describing this market, painting a picture, and telling the story of these women (and those who aspired to be like them), we created a demand where there had been none. We went on to help advertisers in *W* create pictures and tell stories to readers that would bring them into the homes and lives of the most affluent American women. For the Wamsutta sheet account, we worked with an interior designer to use Wamsutta's luxury sheets to decorate the bedroom of a socialite—walls, windows, bed curtains, and pillows. The ad for Wamsutta became, "Where did Bonnie Swearingen sleep last night?"

Stories Remove Barriers and Create Bonds

The standard business transaction occurs across a desk, with the person behind the desk in the superior position to the one seated facing him. When the visitor has an idea to convey, a problem to solve, or an issue to conciliate, the interaction boils down to:

Executive: I don't want to buy anything. Why should I? I'm not interested/I'm busy, and I will think about this later.

Supplicant: I have this to sell to you. I think you'll like it/should do it, and this is how it will benefit you.

Drawing a listener into a pertinent story immediately removes barriers and creates a bond in the same way that going to a movie or a play with someone bonds you with the person who is watching it with you. If the story makes you laugh or engenders sympathy, the decision maker is more receptive to whatever the storyteller is presenting, which is why good speeches begin with personal anecdotes or humor, and why the beginning paragraphs of a novel are so important. The audience, reader, or listener wants to know right away, "Is this person and this presentation worth my time?"

In sales, whether you're selling a product, a service, or an idea, you always create more receptivity by beginning your presentation with a pithy, pertinent story—painting a verbal picture that your listener can "see." This approach works from the very beginning of a conversation where, instead of simply starting with, "Fine, and you?" it is more powerful to say, "I'm having a great day. Clients I've seen today have been thrilled with the performance of their Sales Athletes." Telling a quick story at the outset is a way of creating speed bumps for your presentation. It presets the listener to be receptive to your idea.

A Seven-Point Presentation Structure for Selling Anything

1. Research and then create a picture that fits your point of view.
2. Determine and describe how your client, listener, or prospective buyer fits into the story.
3. Describe why you are there to convey your idea.
4. Describe how your listener will benefit from what you are presenting.
5. Describe how your listener can best use what you are offering.

6. Describe the best way for your listener to purchase or implement your offering.
7. Reiterate the specific benefits of buying and using or implementing what you are offering.

Here's how this presentation structure works with storytelling sales when selling oddly shaped vegetables to a skeptical customer.

1. This carrot is shaped like a bunny rabbit because it comes from seed stock that is more than a hundred years old and originated in France. These carrots are 100 percent natural, grown right here with nothing but water, sunshine, and the good soil of our farm.
2. Most of the produce you buy at the grocery store is not as fresh and costs more.
3. I'm able to share the benefits of this natural produce with you for prices less than you'd pay at the grocery store because we grow it for our family and we can't eat all that we grow.
4. You'll find it's truly delicious and also very healthy because it is so fresh.
5. Please take this recipe for using these vegetables in our favorite soup.
6. If you buy enough for the recipe, you'll need three tomatoes, four carrots, an onion, and a zucchini.
7. I know your family will just love the taste of this soup. You really can't get a healthier meal for less money.

Here's how you might apply the same structure to asking your boss for a raise:

1. When I started working here six months ago, the company leased two airplanes a month, and I was the only person in sales.
2. Since I have been here, your leases have grown to sixteen airplanes a month, and you've had to hire two additional sales representatives to service your accounts—both under my supervision (then show a graph depicting one line moving up to indicate the company's increased revenue, one line remaining flat indicating your compensation).
3. I want to show you how, as revenues have increased, so have my responsibilities.
4. The people you're doing business with have made the following statements about me (offer printed testimonials indicating your value to the company), and here is my ninety-day performance review giving me credit for a substantial share of increased revenues.
5. This is how you can make the best use of my talents and continue exceeding projected revenue goals.
6. My proposal for a fair compensation package is as follows (display a graph showing projected revenues in black and your desired compensation in green to show the fairness of your request for a raise).

7. Just as a reminder, here is my resume, showing you what I brought to the job and what I've accomplished since I've been here.

Rules for Storytelling Selling

Good storytelling sellers always do well in sales, marketing, and communications fields by creating a world of opportunity to bond with others through metaphor, analogy, or humor. I've also seen, as you certainly have, storytellers who sink like stones, with their listeners left feeling awkward, bored, or annoyed. A story that is too long, in questionable taste, or off the point can lose the listener's interest and goodwill.

Research

The Internet puts information about your potential clients and their industries at your fingertips. With just a little extra effort spent doing research, you can gain a broader understanding of your clients' businesses, their successes, marketing strategies, competition, and goals for the future. Pertinent research should guide the story you tell in your presentation.

For example, a Sales Athlete seeking to increase distribution of a line of prepared Mexican food products she represents would start by doing market research. From ACNielsen, the Sales Athlete would find that in a certain geographic area, 495,000 families identify themselves as

Hispanic; yet the grocery chain she is targeting in that area does not sell a broad base of products purchased by those families. She finds that within this trading zone, only one grocer is targeting these families—and sales of prepared Mexican foods by this grocer are stratospheric.

Armed with this research, the Sales Athlete prepares a map of the area, with a bull's-eye highlighting the competitive grocer that is reaching this large, untapped market. She also works with her manager to produce a program for her prospect that will provide coupons and recipes at an in-store sampling to introduce the produce line, as well as banner advertisements of special offers to help stimulate the sell-through of the product line and to generate reorders.

Her story presentation sounds like this:

ACNielsen, the number-one marketing research company in the grocery field, shows how few grocery stores are carrying the food products preferred by the 495,000 Hispanic families located right here in your local retail trading zone. We have a full line of classic Hispanic food products and have developed a program that will drive these customers to your store. (Shows the bull's-eye graphic detailing ACNielsen research to back up her claims.)

To help you attract these highly profitable customers, we have a special promotion that includes in-store sampling, coupons and recipes, and banners for your windows promoting special introductory pricing and letting these customers know you are carrying these convenient products. (Show the outline of the retail program along with the checklist of the full line of products.) As you can see, the upside of our offer is tried-and-true and is backed up by ACNielsen statistics on how much product is moving off the shelves of the other grocers carrying our products. They find these products to be a far more profitable use of designated shelf space. Finally, we will leave you with four free cases today, one case of each of the core products, and ignite our in-store sampling program tomorrow. Would you like me to sign you up today? I'll handle the stocking for you. What do you think?

What are your prospective clients' problems and how will you solve them with what you are presenting? If the problem you are solving is how to gain a competitive advantage, your story should clearly show how your idea helps your listener gain a competitive advantage.

The Internet is an indispensable tool for every Sales Athlete. In accordance with the philosophy, "Always give a little bit of something extra with every endeavor you undertake," time spent on Internet research ensures that your customer has a positive and easy buying experience.

See through the Eye of the Beholder

Before creating your story, see the scenario from the listener's vantage point. What the client has in common with your product, service, or idea is the starting point of your story.

117

What our clients and The Sales Athlete, Inc., service have in common is the goal of increasing sales. I begin any discussion with clients by asking where they are in terms of sales, where they want to be, and what kind of talent they need in order to deliver those goals. I start the story with an anecdote of a noncompetitive company of similar size and similar goals that we have served in the past. It would sound something like this:

> That's interesting that this is the type of talent you're looking for. I had a client with similar goals, and when we placed the first Sales Athlete at that company, the position he filled was driving $690,000 in revenue. Within the first six weeks, the Sales Athlete had invigorated the territory by bringing forth testimonials about how his employer could solve their problems. He sold over $50,000 in new business. This was not by luck; Sales Athletes don't believe in luck. We believe in getting out there and getting the message across to the prospect. That company has since then come back to us and swapped out nonperforming talent for Sales Athletes. If you'd like to call him, here is his telephone number. I have every reason to believe you have all the makings of an equally happy client.

In telling that story, I project listeners to the future. They can verify the picture—of them enjoying the same experience of increased sales—by calling a satisfied client. I told a story that fits what we have in common: their need to make sales and our need to provide solid talent to a solid company.

Create Pictures with Your Words

You've heard it before: "Show, don't tell." The best way to bond with your listener is by describing a scene that your listener can envision.

In meeting with a new client, I hand a piece of paper to the client and ask if she would be kind enough to draw an organization chart for the position she is seeking to fill. While she is going over the org chart, I am able to see the dynamic and vision of the company going forward. I am getting a sense of who that Sales Athlete will be reporting to, the kind of individual and management style. The goal is to identify good managers working in solid companies where the Sales Athlete can do a great job.

Create a Bridge from the Familiar to the New

Use that familiar or easily imagined, comfortable scene to build a logical bridge to the new idea you want to present. I do this with clients by asking them to project themselves twelve months ahead and to look into the rearview mirror at the year just passed. "What exactly do you want your Sales Athlete(s) to have accomplished in this year?" I ask. In projecting them into the future, I'm able to assess how realistic they are as well as what type of talent it will take to reasonably achieve that goal. Then I can say, "Okay, let me describe a couple of Sales Athletes I have in mind who I believe will carry the charge you've laid out over the next twelve months."

In my business there's nothing more powerful than the moment when a client projects himself forward with me to look over our shoulders to what has transpired and to solve those problems in this time frame. Our minds and commitment are focused on solving problems that are a year away. When we go up the corporate ladder to serve company leaders, we move out to five years, seven years, and ten years. Solving their problems is all about finding the right talent, and I see it as a moral obligation to make sure the right people get those jobs.

Rehearse

Never rehearse a story on the listener. Rehearse several times—dozens, if necessary—to become at ease with your story and the timing of your presentation. When people tell me they're not good joke tellers, I know that's because they hear a joke, then try to repeat it to someone a short time later, without having practiced telling the joke first. Is there anything more annoying than someone who is trying to remember a joke *while* they're telling you the joke? If you make a practice of rehearsing jokes ten times into a mirror before telling them, you'd be surprised at how quickly you will become known as a good joke teller. Likewise, to be a good storyteller you have to rehearse.

Keep It Short

Keep it very short and to the point. See what you can shave down or eliminate from your presentation, then go back and pare it down some more. It doesn't take more than thirty seconds to create a vivid picture; and you should be able to build on that picture with supporting facts, anecdotes, and arguments in fewer than three minutes. Don't waste your listener's time by telling a story that has nothing to do with your point simply because you think the story is just too good not to share. The picture you create from the second you begin your presentation should create receptivity to whatever it is you are selling, not distract the listener's focus.

An effective presentation draws a picture of the listener's position, describes the listener benefiting from your idea, and projects the listener into a picture of a future where those benefits are realized.

Too often we make the mistake of thinking that because we speak the same language as the person we are presenting to, anything we say will be clearly understood. Well, if you go to the dictionary and look up the word *frog*, you'll find definitions ranging from buttons to children's games. It's easy to see why people misunderstand each other, particularly if they're meeting for the first time. Stories and verbal pictures help us communicate in a way that fosters clearer understanding and trust, creates receptivity, and moves us closer to consensus.

Sales Athletes are skillful storytellers, and I love hearing their tales about making their strongest sales with the help of storytelling. If you would like to share a great storytelling sales anecdote, please e-mail it to me at kathyaaronson@salesathlete.com.

LET ME LIVE IN THE HOUSE
BY THE SIDE OF THE ROAD
AND BE A FRIEND TO MAN

Part Three

Giving Something Extra

Lesson 7: Give your all at the outset and something extra along the way. Over time, success will be easier than failure.

Lesson 8: There will always be people who have more experience or skills than you do. If you seek them out as mentors and give back to them in return, they will help you reach your goals.

Lesson 9: Career satisfaction and security depend not on the type of work you do, but on the people you work with and the people you serve.

Chapter 7

An Apple for the Road

Nothing succeeds like success; and soon after I opened the Happiness Patch, there were kids trying to sell boxes of produce from their farms on the other side of the road. Their efforts were quickly abandoned, however, because not one was willing to give that something extra that was needed. Walking down the road a mile to plant those signs was the secret to slowing down customers, but it required more effort than most youngsters were willing to expend.

Nothing was different about my produce. What talents or skills did I have that the neighbor kids didn't have? My guess is they just didn't have the same motivation or inclination. They would rather play than connect with the people coming down the road with money to spend. Because I loved meeting those new people, I put extra effort into my speed bumps, presentation, and packaging. I practiced the way I would talk about my vegetables, beginning with, "Let me tell you a story about these tomatoes." I put advance thought into providing value to all types of customers in the way *they* saw value: bargains, promotions, loyalty, or simply a quick and easy transaction. Between sales, I used the time to decorate my paper bags or hand-print recipes for soups and stews that I could put into the bags of those repeat customers with whom I'd developed relationships.

Because of all of these efforts, by the time I actually connected with my customers, doing business was easy! The sales kept coming, and work at the stand didn't feel like work at all. For me, it was play. And to make sure I'd get to keep playing, I never let a customer leave my stand without feeling he or she had been given something extra—a bargain, a special promotion, a recipe, a golden apple for the road.

⤳ LESSON 7 ⤳

Give your all at the outset and something extra along the way. Over time, success will be easier than failure.

People who have reached the pinnacle of success in their careers are those who are able to pick their own projects, working according to the schedule that suits them best and only with the people with whom they like doing business. In my work I come across many of these successful people, and no matter what their business, I consider them to be Sales Athletes. Talk to them about the early days of their careers, and invariably you'll learn that their talents were rewarded with financial and creative freedom only after remarkable effort and sacrifice spent building the foundation for the career they enjoy.

Songwriter Tom Kelly, who wrote many top-of-the-charts songs, including "Like a Virgin," "True Colors," and "So Emotional," knew early in his career that he could continue indefinitely making a decent but not spectacular living playing cover songs in a classy bar band. With a wife and two children to support, it wasn't easy pushing himself to the next level, but every night after work, he'd pour himself some coffee and write long into the night. "I just pushed to grab those extra hours until I got enough songs together to get some attention," Kelly said. Today, he works only with the artists he chooses and focuses only on those songs he believes have a good chance of breaking through. Because of his reputation in the industry as someone who gives his all, he is in great demand.

Giving something extra also worked for best-selling author Norman Bogner. He was working at a television network in England when he wrote his first novel—after work and dinner every night from 9 P.M. to well after midnight while standing up and using a typewriter perched on a highboy dresser in the laundry of his tiny London apartment. His pregnant wife was often ironing on the other side of the same dresser, while their baby slept nearby. With focus and hard work, particularly in those early years, Bogner has written sixteen books that have sold successfully worldwide.

I'm able to pick and choose my clients today because of the years spent building the foundation and reputation of The Sales Athlete. I honed my skills working two and three jobs in New York, during the week selling magazine advertising and on weekends operating an antique stand out of a tiny former appliance store I leased. I scoured the flea markets for quilts, clocks, bronzes, and country furniture—the kind of items I'd grown up with in rural New Hampshire—and sold them as a way not only to pay the rent but also to meet my need to connect with people. And I sure did. Barbra Streisand bought a quilt, Andy Griffith bought a Western bronze, Yoko Ono bought a belt, and tourists grabbed up little alphabet printing blocks I had in a basket up front. There weren't many hours or minutes when I wasn't working, but I loved the way I was making my livelihood because it was also the way I connected in life.

When you give something extra at the outset of any endeavor—whether it's preparing for your presentation with solid research, rehearsal, and crisp materials or building the foundation of your business by working around the clock in the early years—you build a reputation of being someone who works hard and gives your best. Ultimately, this leads you to higher income, more leisure time, and more pride and satisfaction in your life and career.

Giving something extra along the way in your career in order to achieve success might seem a simple and obvious strategy. After all, isn't our culture founded on the work ethic? Yet everywhere, it seems, consumers are frustrated by a failure of business to do their work well and then some.

You've heard the complaints and probably voiced them yourself: poor or no service, salespeople who don't understand the merchandise they're selling, "streamlining" that translates into slightly lower quality, and customer service representatives who know their script but refuse to think their way through a problem that's never before been presented. The employee or sales representative who gives something extra to every endeavor is so rare; in fact, they stand out in sharp contrast to the competition and succeed as a result.

John Lauria was a sales clerk at Williams-Sonoma in Sherman Oaks, California, who happened to answer the phone when a distraught mother of a bride-to-be called with an emergency. The flowers had arrived for her daughter's large wedding the next day, but the carefully chosen, short crystal vases needed for the dinner table centerpieces had been delayed for a week. Williams-Sonoma's Sherman Oaks store had the perfect replacement, but it was already past time for deliveries, and the woman was calling from San Diego, 160 miles away. Lauria himself was about to go home, but instead he told the mother of the bride not to worry. He carefully loaded his car with twenty-two vases and headed south on the freeway. He arrived at the grateful woman's home at 10 P.M. He was just doing what he thought was the right thing—giving something extra to someone in need. His good deed, though, won him an instant promotion and gained for Williams-Sonoma the loyalty of every guest at that wedding.

Giving something extra on a consistent basis is what creates positive word of mouth. Looking and behaving professionally wherever you go is part of this ethic, and so is developing a commitment to excellence. There are many ways that you can incorporate this ethic into the way you do business, without losing money or working yourself ragged, but actually increasing the pleasure in what you do.

A man I know who is a superb negotiator when it comes to buying cars once told me, "If after you buy a car, the dealer throws in free mats, you'll know you've over-paid for the car." My response to him was, "I do business with people all the time, and after we have connected and done our deal, I always give them the equivalent of a golden apple for the road—not because they've paid too much, but because I want to continue the relationship and hope they'll remember me as someone who continually looks out for their best interests, and that includes giving them a little bit of something extra for the journey ahead."

The difference, he explained, is that people who buy cars buy them infrequently, whereas the people who buy my services I hope do so, frequently, over many years. My giving a golden apple for the road extends the relationship, and in my view, that's the most satisfying way to develop and maintain business.

I know that even when it comes to car sales, dealers who operate with integrity and give something extra are often rewarded with the loyalty of customers who return for their next car, their kids' cars, and the repair services of the dealership.

When Mike Weber sold used cars at night and on weekends to pay for his college education, he won a repu-tation of such integrity that his relationships with cus-tomers continued long after he left the car business.

"There were many times where I steered someone away from a particular purchase because it was really not a good idea," Weber recalled. He insisted that cars be in excellent repair and assured his customers they would be fixed, even when his manager wished he wouldn't. If customers longed for a car that would likely cause trouble down the road or didn't see how a less flashy vehicle might serve them better in the long run, Mike would steer them to what he believed was in their best interest. "Ultimately, I'd get thanked to the nth degree!" he recalled. When someone really needed a car but barely missed qualifying for a loan, he helped out, too.

As a result of his giving something extra in those early years of employment and in college, there are still people in his hometown who seek out his advice on car sales, trusting his word and only his word. Mike's commitment to his goal and giving his all to reaching it also earned him top grades in college. He focused like a laser on getting his degree, turning down a great job offering sixty thousand dollars a year plus commissions because it would have interfered with his classes. Few people were aware, at college or on the car lot, that Mike's determination was spurred by a childhood of homelessness.

If you find yourself fearing that you don't have what it takes to succeed, commit to doing your best and more at the outset of every endeavor, build on that commitment, and you will not fail. The commitment to giving something extra is noticed and rewarded, and with it comes credibility you cannot buy.

Ten "Something Extra" Ideas

1. Do What You're Supposed to Do

This concept should not fall under the category of "something extra," but all too often businesses fall short of what should be the baseline expectation: Show up on time, do the work as agreed upon, meet the deadline, do the job completely and well.

2. Maintain Integrity

Just as doing what you're supposed to do when you say you'll do it should be a given, it should go without saying that business ought to be conducted with utmost integrity. However, we read of too many examples of prominent executives cutting corners or stretching ethical boundaries—let alone committing white-collar crimes—to take integrity for granted when doing business. Maintaining impeccable integrity is a value that can transcend barriers of education, language, looks, age, and personality. As anyone who knows the value of an honest car mechanic can attest, integrity in business is golden. It wins loyalty, respect, and, ultimately, success.

3. Provide an Extra Service

Raising the standard of your service by providing something extra is a sure way to win satisfied, loyal customers.

A dry cleaner I know exemplifies this principle. Its employees don't just toss your suit into a machine to be cleaned, then run it through the presser. Every garment that goes into the place is thoroughly inspected. If a button is loose, it'll be sewn back on securely. Hem starting to sag? It'll be expertly stitched. Every garment that leaves the premises is not only cleaned, but in top condition. There will be no surprise missing buttons, broken zippers, or missed stains discovered the hour before your big out-of-town meeting. The result? Despite its higher prices, the cleaner with this policy quickly outgrew its first location and brought a strong referral base as it expanded to three new locations.

4. Offer Information

Simply communicating information that may be common knowledge in your field but that is useful news to your customer or client is a no-stress, no-expense way to rise above the competition. The information can be as casual as, "If you're driving back down Holly Way, be sure to stay at twenty-five miles per hour past the school. Officer Peck waits behind the trees with his radar equipment and loves to give people tickets!" Or it can be sharing a trend observed in your business that may not be common knowledge: real estate prices beginning to flatten, school enrollments up, wine prices rising due to a high rating this season. A free neighborhood map, restaurant recommendations, and a list of services you recommend are all valuable ways to give something extra.

5. Become an Expert

People value, seek out, and pay for expertise. We trust surgeons, even if they can't communicate in our language, if we believe they are experts in their specialty. You don't have to have a Ph.D. to gain expertise in a narrow aspect of your field; you just need to conscientiously seek training, read regularly, connect with other experts, and stay current with information. When you are the go-to person on a specific subject, whether it's Chinese trade, the history of the paper shredder in the marketplace, or the technological tools used by your clients, that expertise lends you interest and credibility. Expertise—even if not directly tied to your clients' business—offers another reason for people to seek you out in business.

6. Stay Current

Keeping up-to-date with developments in your field and staying aware of events in the news and your community are means to maintaining your credibility. You'll be viewed as someone to trust and seek out for information if you are well read, on top of things, and able to make meaningful connections between developments in your business and the lives of people around you. You'll be the first to let people know of a helpful new product, service, or resource, and clients will appreciate that they can call you to find out what's up. Take time each day to read your trade magazines and journals, and read a credible newspaper for articles that go beyond sound bites. Attend the trade shows not only of your own business but also of your most important clients to keep current your understanding of their needs.

Staying current with technology, the culture around you, and the materials you use in your presentation also provides credibility that can buffer you from ageism in your career. People aren't viewed as dinosaurs in the workplace simply because of their age. Ageism is real, but it most often works against the people who refuse to stay professionally fit. If you fail to stay current with the people you report to and persist in using the tools, language, and procedures of an era gone by, you'll be sidelined in your career regardless of your age. I've seen people in their twenties who are already brittle and set in their ways and Sales Athletes in their sixties who are always excited and knowledgeable about the latest books, movies, equipment, and trends. Their presentations are cutting-edge, and so are their ideas. Staying current requires agility and persistence, but the satisfaction it brings is well worth the effort.

7. Keep Training

A commitment to regular training will build your credibility, expand and improve your professional relationships, and help you avoid injuries to your career. There's nothing wrong with admitting you don't know something, but a refusal to learn about new methods, technologies, skills, or industry trends clearly identifies you to clients and employers as someone who's just marking time and unwilling to give anything extra. Staying professionally fit through training means reading your trade publications as well as the publications of your best clients. Don't wait for the annual meeting to attend the workshops or seminars that will add to the knowledge you can offer to clients or customers.

The reason we call Sales Athletes by that name is because of their commitment to professional fitness and to continuous training in every aspect of their lives. To stay on top of their game, they stay abreast of what's going on in the world, remain curious, and ask questions even when in social situations, always on the lookout for best practices: "How can I be more successful? Healthier? What's the best new equipment? Who's out there giving the best negotiation training?" They are satisfied with life and love their careers, and in order to maintain that level of satisfaction, they know they must embrace growth.

In a survey of advertising salespeople, The Sales Athlete, Inc., found that those with poor-to-average returns spent just 2 percent of their time on tasks considered to be self-improvement, while the most successful Sales Athletes spent 10 percent of their time on self-improvement. That 10 percent of the day wasn't necessarily spent sitting in a classroom, but it included listening to tapes and reading books while traveling and waiting—another habit of people committed to staying in professional shape.

8. Offer Introductions and Contacts

There is no more valuable information than that that connects one person to another for a positive purpose. Whether it's a list of reliable babysitters given to a client who's new in town, the name of an expert handyman, or the rundown on the vice president at a company in charge of a project that would benefit your client, providing contacts is an invaluable way of giving something extra. Because relationships in business are so important, however, contact names, references, or introductions should never be given casually. There are times when giving something extra means protecting your relationships and times when opening relationships to others is the most generous and helpful thing you can do.

Your credibility is on the line when you send new people to business contacts you have developed and nurtured in the course of doing business. It's important that you respect and view as credible the person seeking a contact; and before you provide that contact, you must believe the person truly has something valuable to offer.

9. Stay Consistent

Giving something extra on a consistent basis is what creates positive word of mouth. Like it or not, people are watching, making determinations and judgments all the time. Even the transactional person you think you'll never

see again can spread the good word about your professional behavior and positive attitude in ways you may
never know. Consistently doing your best and consistently
minding your manners help you build credibility. Nobody's
perfect, but those who understand the power of consistency and work hard to maintain high standards at all
times are more likely to be given slack when they slip because they are known as people who rarely falter.

Conversely, a Jekyll-and-Hyde personality, or someone who is capable of brilliance one moment but subpar
performance the next, is simply not trustworthy in business. Success-driven managers want and deserve to know
whom they are dealing with and what consistent standard
of work they can expect.

10. Be Generous

Generosity of spirit engenders trust and enhances credibility. If you approach all life as a zero-sum game—with-
holding information, keeping "score" in every petty
encounter, investing energy in pennies spent rather than in
dollars earned—others will believe you've nothing extra to
give. I'm not talking about profligacy—foolish overspend-
ing or giving away the store—but simple generosity that
comes from confidence in knowing there's enough to go
around, that giving something to others doesn't reduce
your "share" but benefits you as well as the recipient.
There are so many opportunities to be generous beyond
giving something extra in the ways I've listed.

A friend who is a movie buff, for example, and lets you know that the well-reviewed blockbuster you are thinking of seeing "is a good airplane movie or a renter" has generously saved you time and money.

Replenish—So You'll Have Something Extra to Give

As important as it is to extend yourself by giving something extra, it is equally important to recognize the need for balance and replenishment so you can give what it takes to succeed. Successful people don't ignore their own needs for family relationships, friendships, exercise, and rest. Even if you love your work, and I hope you do, don't forget to replenish yourself at the end of each day and to give something extra to yourself along the way. As you plow through a particularly difficult project or face the pressure of a deadline, give yourself permission to postpone some daily chores. Take a walk with your family instead of rushing to wash the dishes. Enjoy a good workout, or listen to your favorite music before bed. You'll find that just a few minutes a day of whatever brings you peace and replenishment will help you stay focused and enthusiastic about your work. Failure to replenish will sap you of the joy in what you do, and without that, there is no success.

Chapter 8

An Apple for the Teacher

I had the best attitude and work ethic a little girl in rural New Hampshire could have had, and my fruits and vegetables were as fresh and nutritious as could be. The Happiness Patch would've been an unhappy and unsuccessful venture, however, if it weren't for the help of Miss August, the kind teacher who dressed like Lois Lane and taught me about slowing down traffic and presenting my produce in an appealing way. My work is the fulfillment of my dream, and achieving it has taken more than a desire to connect and willingness to work hard. Beginning with Miss August, I've benefited from the wise counsel and gentle prodding of mentors.

Today, I'm a "rent-a-mentor" to people starting, changing, and reinvigorating their careers. Young people I've mentored have gone on to become Sales Athletes and CEOs who have referred me to important clients. I am reminded daily of the value of seeking help from people who know more than you know whenever you set out on a new endeavor.

As I grew, I found mentors ranging from Helen Gurley Brown, editor in chief of *Cosmopolitan* magazine, to O. B. Bond, an impeccable gentleman and stellar publisher who

---

> ## ⌒ LESSON 8 ⌒
>
> There will always be people who have more experience or skills than you do. If you seek them out as mentors and give back to them in return, they will help you reach your goals.

taught me how to add polish to my rural upbringing and to negotiate the social and business protocols so foreign to a young woman like me. I knew I could benefit from the example and advice of others and worked hard to overcome the fear of asking for it. One day, very early in my career in media advertising sales, I was riding the elevator between the floors of the great agency, Ogilvy & Mather, when the door opened and there I saw Malcolm Forbes. When he nodded a polite, "Hello," I blurted out, "Mr. Forbes! My name is Kathy Aaronson, and I'm one of the first women to sell national advertising. What's the secret to success in advertising sales?" I was quaking like a leaf.

"You have to believe in what you're selling," he said and handed me his business card as the elevator door closed. Later, I gathered all my courage to call him for advice, and from the moment he took my call, I was devoted to this great man. He was a great mentor to young people in advertising, and I got the sense he enjoyed sharing his knowledge.

In helping people transition to new careers, the cornerstone of our work at The Sales Athlete, Inc., is to help talented people establish relationships with mentors. A vision and the willingness to start a new career or enhance an existing career aren't enough. You need people to help you get where you need to go. Mentors are the people who support you in the beginning of your journey to a new or different career, who help you meet the people you need to know to succeed.

How to Find a Mentor

If you are sincere, focused, and willing to give back something extra as you search for a mentor, you'll find that most people are kind enough to be willing to help you reach your goals. If you fear taking the first step toward seeking a mentor, remember that mentoring is a two-way street. In asking for help, you must be willing to give back to your mentor at every opportunity, both in the appreciation you express and in the information, contacts, or assistance you can provide as you grow in your career. Don't forget that in a two-way mentor relationship, your own achievements can help validate your mentor's success, and you can provide your mentor with valuable insights into a different age group. So please don't be stopped by thinking, "she's far too busy and important to talk to me." Even if you're not fortunate enough to see your ideal mentor on an elevator, there are many other ways you can connect with role models, get solid advice, or develop meaningful mentor relationships.

Reach Out in Writing

You can start with a simple letter:

> Dear Director/Producer/Engineer/President of an ar-
> chitectural firm [whatever career arena that fits your
> dream]:
>
> I'm in the process of a career change/graduating
> from XYZ University, and in order to succeed with this
> endeavor, I need to connect with someone who has
> been successful in [this endeavor]. Would you be kind
> enough to spend a few minutes with me? I can come
> to your office or speak with you over the telephone,
> and in return for your guidance, I will look for all the
> big and little ways I can say "Thank you" throughout
> my career, because you will have helped me during
> the most difficult time—when I was getting started.
>
> Sincerely, . . .

Attend Networking Meetings

Go to the association or networking meeting of the people
with whom you'd like to work. Take your resume, wear a
smile, and be positive, friendly, and clear that you're there
because you want to meet people who are doing the thing
you want to do. Say honestly that you're hoping one of
them will be kind enough to spend a few minutes with you
for guidance. You'd be surprised how willing people are to

assist you. The most powerful word in the English language is: "Help!" Don't be afraid to ask for it.

Assist at Work

Offering to help is another way to find a mentor. The question, "How can I help you?" can open doors. If you see your manager beleaguered, ask if you can do anything to help. Even if she pushes you back on the first attempt, you've created a building block for a good relationship by establishing yourself as a person who is eager to help and learn.

Volunteer

Go to the association meeting of the industry with which you'd like to associate , and offer to volunteer, even in menial tasks. Explain that you'd love to work in the industry and want to learn through assisting. What does this accomplish? It puts you right in the arena where prospective employers can see you and form positive impressions of who you are, and it puts you in the presence of potential mentors.

Rent a Mentor

You can also rent a mentor by hiring a professional career coach or by offering to pay for the time of an expert in an area where you need career development, personal polish, or relationship skills.

Follow Role Models

If you have in mind a high-profile person whom you dream of as a mentor but who won't or can't give you any time, you can still follow his or her example by reading articles, speeches, or profiles. Do some Internet research, and collect the wisdom of people who are experts in the field you want to master. Make a file of written materials that provide helpful examples of how others have succeeded, and refer to it whenever you feel the need for inspiration.

My earliest role models were intrepid redheads Brenda Starr, the comic book news reporter, and Lucille Ball, who would get herself into a jam on every show, but picked herself up, dusted herself off, and was upbeat and ready for another day.

Long before Helen Gurley Brown actually became my role model, I saw her on TV and related to her because she, too, had a rural background and clearly had to overcome nervousness when she appeared on *The Merv Griffin Show*. In her magazine, the first for working women, she became my fashion guidepost, my insight into helpful and important books of the day and into workplace issues. She was a great role model for young, single, working women living in major metropolitan cities, and I couldn't believe my good fortune when I actually had the opportunity to work for her.

Often a role model might be willing to talk to you at lunch or on the phone once or twice, but not to enter into a long-term mentoring relationship. Don't take it personally, and be grateful and appreciative of any time given. Understand that long-term mentoring relationships are special, and don't confuse them with social friendships or parental or sibling relationships.

Your father, mother, clergyman, sister, or best friend may not hesitate to give you advice, but they may not want to challenge you, hurt your feelings, or welcome your growth in ways that are unfamiliar to them.

The characteristics of a good mentor are:

- Has a track record of success and more experience than you do in the area in which you need mentoring.
- Is willing to listen and actually hear what you are saying.
- Has no blind spot when it comes to you, and is willing to give you unvarnished, truthful perceptions and advice about what steps you must take to reach your goals.
- Is kind and caring but will not do your work for you.
- Expects you to follow up on any advice given, even if you decide for some reason not to take it.
- Gives you a deadline for your step-by-step plan, and stays in touch along the way to see that you've taken those steps.
- Is patient with the process of your growth.

- Recognizes that the hardest part of anything is getting started, and challenges you to take the steps you need to take to get your progress under way.
- Has faith in you, and lets you know he or she believes in you.

When you seek help from someone more experienced than you, be willing to truly listen to what he or she says, even if it's not exactly what you'd hoped to hear. An adviser may suggest you take several difficult steps rather than the shortcut you'd wished for.

At times I have had to turn down a request for mentoring because the person seeking my advice was pursuing a profession in which he or she wouldn't be successful or was aspiring to something unrealistic based on his or her skills or economic reality. A few years ago, for example, a man drove to my office in a Rolls Royce—one that was in such need of repair that we could hear it clanking and sputtering from a block away.

The man had once been flying high as a top executive in an industry that was dying due to a combination of changes in tax laws, regulations, and the economy. He'd been out of work for more than a year and hiding the fact by persisting in living the life of a millionaire, driving a car he could not afford to repair, and avoiding close contact with anyone from his old life. By the time he came to my office, he was living on health bars and was soon to lose his outsized house. Nonetheless, he wanted me to find him a placement as president of a company in the same industry he'd left, earning the same amount he once earned, even though the industry he came from really no longer existed.

I told him what he did not want to hear: He needed to remanufacture himself. After his anger subsided, he took his first step and followed my advice by calling all his friends and asking them for leads on any kind of project work that would get him both involved with people and out in the business world. One of his friends happened to be a lawyer who needed someone as smart as he was but who was willing to pay him only an hourly rate plus commissions to collect the settlements reached by the law firm for its clients. By taking this job that was far "beneath" anything he'd considered when walking into my office, the man in the Rolls not only got himself back on his feet financially, but also went on to a successful new career in a related field.

Even when an adviser gives you counsel that is tough to swallow or that you decide not to follow, it's important that you acknowledge it promptly. And when a role model agrees to give the gift of mentoring, understand that mentoring is a two-way street.

How to Keep a Mentor

- Do your homework. Don't ask for someone's valuable time until you've learned everything you can about that person and the work he or she does. If the prospective mentor has written articles or given speeches about the topic you're interested in, read them before you ask questions.

- Send along information or news that might be helpful to your mentor.
- Defend the good name of your mentor. If anything negative is ever said about your mentor, point out how helpful the mentor has been to you.
- Always look for the big and little ways to say "thank you."
- Recognize and acknowledge the critical role played by the mentor in every step of your success.

Noted career counselor Adele Scheele shared a powerful story about a brief mentoring session that occurred by happenstance. She was sitting on an airplane and feeling blue, she recalled. It was around the Christmas holidays. An important business appointment had been cancelled, and she was heading home. Seated next to her was a man who'd been a leader in the Teamsters union—a heavy man in poor health whose wife had recently died. He, too, seemed to be at the end of his rope.

"When I was blue, hearing other people's stories allowed me to go in a different direction," Adele said. "So I asked about how he built his union, and his stories were amazing to me. Forgetting my troubles, I took out a pencil and paper and gave him a plan for how he could refresh his career by teaching high school and college students this fascinating history of the labor movement. By the end of the flight, I felt renewed; I was freshened. I could go back home, and the world would not end. It didn't matter whether my venture 'took' or not. I'd just go back and do it again." But the work she had done did "take," and in short order she had a new book, a radio talk show, profiles in major newspapers, and several lucrative speaking engagements. Not long afterward, her airplane companion wrote her a note saying he was following her plan and thanking her for saving his life; he had been flying west to say good-bye to his son, fully intending suicide.

Dear Mentor —
Thank you so much for being there when I was first getting started. — Kathy

Instead, his life took a new direction because of career guidance offered by a professional mentor on an airplane.

Top performers recognize that if they don't have mentors, they will stay at the same level in their career. The people above you are the ones who help you move to their level. So if you are not happy standing still, move forward by finding, following, appreciating, and giving back to your mentors.

If I could only give one piece of advice about how to reach your goal, this is it: Seek the help of people who know more than you know whenever you set out on a new endeavor—and don't forget to say "thank you."

Chapter 9

It's All about the People

The motivation that led to the Happiness Patch and to every one of my endeavors since then was a strong desire to connect with people. In my first business venture, the vegetables were secondary. Although I saw their value as a product, their real value to me was as a means to connect with the people driving by in their beautiful Fords, Chevrolets, and Buicks. I wanted to meet them. If I could have made those connections as easily by selling popcorn instead of vegetables or repairing tires instead of selling anything, either enterprise would have been fine; it was the interaction I needed and wanted.

That need to connect grew and became more focused as I came into adulthood. I found ways to meet interesting people by offering unusual items for sale to customers who were a fascinating mix of actors, financiers, bohemians, and businesspeople. I later found work that would put me into contact with top performers in a broad range of fields—from publishers to designers and manufacturers. I decided I wanted to spend my life around these people, and I could imagine no greater satisfaction than solving their problems while sharing with others what I'd learned about success. I began coaching people who were looking for ways to live profitable, prosperous lives and were looking everywhere for great communicators with integrity and drive. When I found them, I provided every service I could to prepare them for the next step and to connect them with solid managers, working for terrific companies for which they could do a great job and that would compensate and appreciate them appropriately.

For me, it's always been about the people. I quickly learned that it didn't matter whether I was selling produce, antiques, magazine ads, or The Sales Athlete, Inc., services. What I wanted was a career where I could meet interesting, successful people and develop ongoing, mutually satisfying business relationships with them over time.

ꝰ LESSON 9 ꝰ

Career satisfaction and security depend not on the type of work you do, but on the people you work with and the people you serve.

The more relationships you build in your career, the more likely you are to move to a job where you already have a relationship with the people who have hired you. The interview question won't be "How will you work out?" but "What relationships will you bring?" "What equipment will you need?"

Today my produce stand on the side of the road is The Sales Athlete, Inc. My products are the masterful communicators who bring products, services, and ideas to the business world and who live lives that are both profitable and balanced.

People come to our service because they are seeking to change careers or to enhance existing careers or because they are confused college graduates uncertain about how to apply to the workplace what they studied in school. Often, people spend many unhappy years making decisions based on the labels that were on the buildings of their college campus: engineering, history, life sciences, law. They've chosen a major because they're interested in, or perhaps their parents steered them toward, a subject area, and then they persist in pursuing a career based on that subject area, whether or not their personality fits any job that might exist with that subject in its title.

How to Choose a Career You'll Love

Often, when I ask people to describe their dream job and then to explain to me why they don't have it now, their response is, "I have to pay the rent." "I have kids to support." "I need to pay off my college loans." And I tell them the truth: "You can work with the people you want to work with *and* make the money you want to make *and* pay your bills. Right now, however, you don't know the people who will get you to the places you want to go. So let me help you find those people."

Even people who find their dream job right out of college will find change in that job inevitable. In fact, by age forty, over 70 percent of all college graduates are in professions that no longer are related to their original academic focus. Relationships they've made in college, however, frequently last a lifetime. The same is true in your career.

My prescription for a lifetime of professional success is based on asking yourself the following questions:

- What types of people do I want to spend a professional lifetime with?
- What types of services could I provide to these people?

If you target your associations and build professional relationships by providing valuable services to the types of people you enjoy, you will create career equity that will see you through economic downturns, changes in your industry, downsizings, mergers, and moves. *It's not what you know, but who knows what you know that determines your vocational security.*

Take your skill sets and match them to an industry that is populated by the types of people you'd invite over for dinner. This approach not only can make your job more satisfying, but is beneficial because these people are the ones who will carry you through life. When we view career options through the lens of subject matter, we feel our options are limited. When we realize it's all about the people, the world opens wide.

A man who came to one of my seminars was a drummer who had spent twenty-five years on the road with successful bands but decided to leave the music industry behind when he married and had a child. He got a job as a soda truck delivery driver close to home, but it was grueling work and he hated it. After my seminar, when I went to shake his hand, this man met my eyes with a scowl. "All this stuff about the people," he snarled. "I can't work in the music business without going on the road, and that's a rough life of no family. I'm not messing up my family to stay in the music business; so, according to you, I've wasted twenty-five years of my life!" I could see the pain behind his anger, and I agreed to consult with him privately the next day.

"How did you spend your spare time during those twenty-five years when you *weren't* drumming?" I asked when we met. He explained that when he was on tour, most of his offstage hours were spent in video arcades, where his hobby was decoding the electronic games, challenging himself to win by spending the fewest number of quarters possible. Then he'd write articles for gaming magazines telling readers the secrets to the games.

"I am 'The Game Wizard,'" he said, giving me the pen name that was known by video and arcade gaming aficionados.

I went online and found a directory of electronic game manufacturers, two of which were within ten miles of his home. Those were the companies he should target for employment.

"I don't have business experience; I just know all about their games," he protested.

"Don't you understand?" I asked. "That's exactly why they *need* you!" In the course of doing what he loved in his spare time, this man had built a national network of relationships and had inside information about how these people buy their machines. These people were to these gaming firms the most valuable customers: owners of video arcades all over America. He rewrote his resume to focus less on his work as a musician and more on how he had become an insider in the field of video gaming. In fairly short order, he went to work with one of the major game manufacturers, where he was happily and lucratively employed before creating his own business, specializing in putting celebrities—beginning with the musicians he'd worked with—into arcade games. Both career transitions were made smoothly because of the people this man had connected with, even though at first he didn't realize the power of the connections he had.

Jobs aren't consistent, but people are. Imagine you can project yourself into the future and look in the rearview mirror. The one constant you would see in a lifetime full of changes would be the people you have done business with. As industries change, successful people change with them, bringing along with them the professional associations of people they can depend on and respect professionally.

A podiatrist I know had a dream job as a dancer with a respected national ballet company, but he recognized that his employability would end by his late twenties. He pursued training in podiatry, with a practice that caters especially to dancers. He is able to work around the people he loves—dancers—by giving them a service he is uniquely qualified to provide. Rather than waiting for his career to end, this man wisely moved it forward based on

159

the people he wanted to associate with throughout his long life.

How do you build your career around the kind of people you want to be with, no matter what your interest or expertise? When people approach me for career coaching, I ask them to consider any new job prospect based on the following five questions:

1. *What is the dress code?*

What do the people look like on the job, and how are their most profitable customers or clients dressed? Is it strictly a pinstriped, buttoned-down environment; a more casual setting; or one where artistic flair is on display? Answers to this question will not only guide you on your interview attire but also tell you something about how you'd fit in.

2. *Who are the people you'd interact with?*

Will you be part of a team? Who else is on the team, and what do they do? Will you be dealing with clients from a variety of industries or just one, with outside clients or only people in your office?

3. *What is the means of interaction?*

Will you be cold-calling prospective new clients on the telephone or in person? Will you stay in your office, or will you see clients and customers on the road?

4. *What are the day-to-day tasks?*

Will you be doing predictable tasks each day? Is the job a deadline-a-minute, intense and unpredictable; or is it a pretty reliable, steady mix of administrative chores and communications tasks? Try to break down exactly what a day, a week, and a month would look like in the position you're considering; and ask yourself exactly how your experience to this point prepares you to do those tasks.

5. *What is the culture of this business?*

Is this an entrepreneurial environment where everyone is expected to work creatively and independently on behalf of the team? Are there great resources available, or must you provide your own? Is it hierarchical, where everyone has an assigned role and is expected to adhere to clear lines of authority both above and below?

When you know the answer to these questions, you will be able to discern whether the job is one that will help you build a foundation of business relationships that will serve you in the future. If you decide you want the job, knowing the answers to these questions will help you to move past fear in the job interview and to respond confidently to the prospective employer's questions based on the same five criteria. You'll know exactly how and where you'd fit on the job and how your experience has prepared you to succeed. You will be able to describe how you would succeed by matching both experience and enthusiasm for the people you'll be interacting with, the way you'll be interacting with them, the tasks you'll be asked to do each day, and the corporate culture you'll be entering.

I've seen a researcher's pie chart showing ten different ways an employer can find someone to fill a job, including the classified ads, executive recruiters, networking meetings, and resumes sent in the mail. On this pie chart, 51 percent of the time employers say they would prefer to hire someone through the recommendation of a trusted business associate. That trusted associate of your dream employer could be your Uncle Fred, your next-door neighbor, or the father of your best tennis buddy.

What does that tell you? It's important never to abuse the confidence of friends or relatives or to behave in a way that will lead anyone to mistrust your judgment. Your future boss could be watching. For example, by getting drunk at the block party or disrespecting Uncle Fred at Thanksgiving dinner, you could be foreclosing an opportunity to be recommended for that dream job. You want to behave in such a manner that anyone who knows you would feel comfortable recommending you for a great job.

When you do your work well and with integrity, people notice. You will benefit from the tremendous power of positive word of mouth.

Tobias Buschmann arrived in this country from Germany in 1984, with one telephone number and no cash. He managed to get work with MCM, a luxury luggage company based in Germany, where eventually he was given the assignment of handling manufacturing in Asia and sales in Japan. The job brought him contacts in high fashion houses around the world, with Asian sources for raw materials and buyers in Japan. He had many loyal clients and colleagues with whom he had built a solid reputation for being reliable, consistent, ethical, and dedicated to the highest quality. Over time, Buschmann also developed an eye for talent and an ability to sense which of the many up-and-coming designers might become the next fashion sensation.

Suddenly, however, MCM went out of business, and Buschmann was out of a job. Rather than find a new employer, he focused all of his resources on a venture that would allow him to work with and for the people he loved. Today, Buschmann is CEO of YZ, Inc., a New York–based company that finds young designers with companies doing five hundred thousand to three million dollars worth of business and who have great creative talent but who lack business acumen. YZ, Inc., puts these designers in contact with its manufacturing sources, addresses any business or organizational problems they may be experiencing, and helps them get international exposure through vendors in Japan. Today, Buschmann enjoys tremendous business success and the grateful loyalty of some of fashion's most celebrated names.

"I built this little niche," he said. "I put all my efforts toward really building an impeccable reputation of not accepting failure and bringing this talent to these resources, and over the last twenty years, these resources have depended on me to bring this kind of business to them." Buschmann embodies the power of giving something extra and of building a career based on loyal relationships.

Career Security through Thick and Thin

Even if you don't like your present job, your co-workers, who respect and recognize your worth, are valuable to you and your future. You, too, will realize your career has always been about the people. Brad Davis, vice president of sales and marketing for the Walt Disney Marketing Group, calls it the "trotline of business relationships."

"In every job I've had, every position I've held, I've brought at least one person from the company I'd worked for previously," he explained. "Sometimes I've brought multiple people I had worked with throughout my career. Successful businesspeople throughout their careers develop what we called in Arkansas 'fishing with a trotline': You spool out a line, just troll with it, keep moving along, and this line with lots of hooks in it gathers up the catch as you go about doing other things on the boat that day. You pull in the trotline. You develop relationships on your business trotline and bring them along throughout your career in different professions, different jobs, and different scenarios. . . . You don't go out and say, 'I'm going to develop two protégés today.' But over time you might have had five people who worked for you, two different clients, a person you did business with, and you mentor them and they mentor you, and you wind up supporting each other throughout your careers."

The trotline only works if you do business with the people you *like* doing business with and pay attention to nurturing professional relationships by mentoring, respecting your mentors, and remembering to be a professional twenty-four hours a day.

Epilogue

The Most
Important People

In the course of training more than two hundred people a week and recruiting for corporations ranging from online start-ups to major entertainment networks, I have been struck by the similarities in the way the happiest and most successful people do business. When I ask these people—the people I call Sales Athletes—to look back to their childhoods for the first experience that drove them to sell, persuade, or negotiate to get what they needed, most of them cited two to five years of business experiences before the age of twelve.

My story of kid courage leading to a successful first business, and of the same motivation that gave me kid courage nurturing a long career, is not unusual. The president of a Fortune 500 company today uses the same skills she first developed when administering her brother's neighborhood circus. When I asked an editor of an alternative newspaper what her business experience was before the age of twelve, she claimed she didn't have any. When pressed, however, she revealed that in return for helping her sister with her spelling, she received an extra dollar in her allowance!

Others have performed for the praise of their parents or learned to develop a talent to win the acceptance of peers. Often, the sheer joy of accomplishment as a child is enough to make us overcome obstacles and give our utmost to develop our skills.

I encourage you to look back to your childhood and find your kid courage. What was the seed that motivated you? If you find yourself in a less-than-satisfying life situation, unmotivated or unappreciated in your work, perhaps you've failed to nurture that seed with the equivalent of sunshine, water, or good soil.

It's never too late to apply the lessons of the Golden Apple to your career, to carefully tend your garden so that the seeds of excellence within you will thrive and you will produce to your maximum potential. I hope you will now be confident in finding and determining your value, in identifying the mentors who will support your growth, and in locating the perfect sunny spot that will allow you to thrive. You should be able to effectively slow people down enough to give your ideas the attention they deserve and to present your ideas in a way that will engage your listeners as powerfully as a great storyteller would. Most of all, I hope you will always remember the importance of giving something extra and of using the fruits of your labor to give back to others, because your ability to succeed is always all about the people.

I've told you that connecting with people was my motivation for opening the Happiness Patch and for every business venture between then and the founding of The Sales Athlete, Inc. Now, I'd like you to know my motivation for wanting to connect with you. I wrote this book not only because I wanted to share what I know will help you become more successful, but also because when you do well at your work, the seeds of your success stimulate our economy and help to create jobs. Job creators are the most important people in the world. When you bring new products, services, or ideas to the marketplace, when you help your employer build and thrive, you become a job creator. And when you create jobs, you improve lives and strengthen communities in the process.

I believe we all have a moral obligation to do what we can to succeed in our own lives so we'll have the ability to improve the lives of others. By becoming a Sales Athlete, you take that obligation seriously and really do create success, not only for yourself but also for the people you work for, mentor, and inspire in your career. *You* are the most important people there are. Please enjoy this apple, with my compliments, for the road ahead.

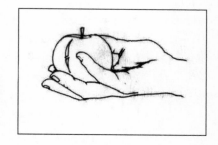

Appendix

The Golden Apple
Action Plan

∽ LESSON 1 ∽

A crooked carrot can be as valuable as a golden apple. To get what you want, you must first learn how what you have is of value to others.

Checklist for Determining the Value of Anything

Before you present your product, service, or idea, determine its value to others.

1. Does it meet a demand?
2. Does it save time and/or effort?
3. Does it carry authority?
4. Does it convey credibility?
5. Does it provide value by association?
6. Does it offer a positive experience?

Nothing Happens Until You Learn How to Sell Yourself

Assess your own value using the same checklist you'd use for determining the value of your product, service, or idea. If you feel weak in any area of the checklist, you'll know where to focus your training. And if you understand and appreciate your own value, you'll be credible in conveying the value of your product, service, or idea.

- In what ways do your skills meet the demand in the workplace? Is there a demand you can fill that nobody is meeting?
- How will your product, service, or idea save time or effort?
- In what ways can you claim authority?
- In what ways do you convey credibility?
- What associations do you have that will be of value to others?
- Are you a positive person with whom other people *enjoy* doing business?

⤷ LESSON 2 ⤶

People have busy lives. If you want them to be receptive to your product, service, candidacy, or idea, you first need to create "speed bumps" to slow them down.

The Five-Touch Technique

When beginning a business relationship with someone new, be prepared to preset their receptivity to your product, service, or idea by using five "speed bumps." To be effective, speed bumps must be consistent and tell a story. They should cause your listener to:

1. Notice.
2. Slow down enough to pay attention.

3. Become interested.
4. Want to hear more.

Once you have built credibility and begun to build a rapport with those steps, your listener should:

5. Be receptive during your proposal.

VERBAL SPEED BUMPS

- Notes.
- Postcards.
- E-mails.
- Voice-mail messages: brief, clear, credible, repeating the key message in a previous e-mail or note.
- Article or testimonial about your service, with a brief note that says you believe the recipient will also benefit from giving you a few minutes of his or her time.

PREMIUM SPEED BUMPS Inexpensive, clever, or useful items can help you deliver your message and convey your dedication to getting across the value of your idea. When you follow up with a call to the recipient (your next speed bump), you will be remembered as the person who sent the cleverly packaged message. Be certain the speed bump is tailored to your audience. Some examples of speed bumps that I've used:

- A blue ribbon "winner" button.
- A valentine at Christmastime, looking ahead.
- A lottery ticket: "Take a chance!"
- A beautifully wrapped packet of seeds, with a message that your idea will help their business grow.
- "Message in a bottle."

⤳ LESSON 3 ⤳

To create receptivity with the greatest number of people, be prepared to do business in a way that makes them comfortable.

The Four Universal Types of Customers

The people who approach you in business are likely to fall into one of four categories. You'll have fewer disappointments and suffer less rejection if you learn to recognize each type and are prepared to provide your product, service, or idea in a way that brings satisfaction to each type.

QUICK AND EASY   These people need a fast, painless transaction that will let them quickly move on to the other activities in their busy lives.

- Don't take an extra second of their time.
- Make their life easier by making the transaction smooth.

- Don't take it personally if they are distracted.
- Don't try to engage in unnecessary conversation.

BARGAIN HUNTERS These people are only satisfied if they believe they've gotten good value at a price lower than what other people are paying.

- Always have a lower-cost option available.
- Appreciate them for what they are: customers.

PROGRAM LOVERS These people receive satisfaction from regular repeat service, membership deals, and packages with perks.

- Create ways for program lovers to project the cost and profit of your product or service over time.
- Offer incentives for customers to give you their repeat business, and treat them as members of your inner circle who get extra benefits for their loyalty.

RELATIONSHIPS These customers see doing business with you as part of a relationship.

- Engage in the relationship, move it forward, and treasure it, letting it be known how much you do.
- Treat a business relationship like a member of your corporate family.

- Call on these relationships to bounce new ideas off them and to get feedback on business practices.
- Never forget that relationships are the key to career security and financial success.

ᴄ᷉ LESSON 4 ᴄ᷉

To overcome fear of rejection, learn how to recognize and to communicate with six types of prospects.

When it comes time to ask for what you want—whether it is to win support for an idea or to sell a product or service—the people you approach will respond in one of six ways. Once you recognize this and prepare to meet each of these responses with confidence, you will have overcome the biggest obstacle to success: fear of rejection.

Six Possible Responses to Your Approach

1. Rude
   - Don't take it personally.
   - Separate yourself from all the people who have disappointed them.
2. Indifferent
   - Use speed bumps.
   - Differentiate yourself from the people who have wasted their time.

3. Skeptical
   - Don't be defensive; prepare a Skeptic Emergency Kit.
   - Have three absolute truths—research, testimonial, and a guarantee—to remove skepticism and to win trust.

4. Interested
   - Don't forget to tell your story.
   - Find out specifically why they are interested; try to understand their needs and expectations, and address them one by one.

5. Indefinite
   - Lead the way.
   - Ask questions to bring any objections out into the open, such as, "If I were looking for your best interests between now and February, what would you suggest I look for on your behalf?" or "With what you know about your partner and how he makes decisions, what would you suggest I include in my presentation?"

6. Objector
   - Appreciate the value of a person who clearly states what he or she wants and needs.
   - Be prepared to meet objections in advance: Can you offer a different payment plan or a lower cost alternative? Can you tailor your service more specifically to the anticipated needs of this person?

∽ LESSON 5 ∽

A good presentation adds credibility and value to anything you have to offer, including yourself.

The 24-Hour Professional

Nothing you wear, say, or project should limit receptivity to what you are presenting.

- How do the most profitable customers of your clients dress? Take your wardrobe tips from them.
- Brush up on manners by reading business and social etiquette books and articles.
- Attitude check: Remember your next employer may be watching.

Packaging Counts

- Be willing to spend more for presentation materials that are crisp and clear and that convey credibility.
- Stay up-to-date on presentation technology that will improve your ability to communicate your message.

> ∽ **LESSON 6** ∽
>
> Stories have the power to break down walls and to open
> doors to receptivity.

A Seven-Point Presentation Structure for Selling Anything

1. Research, and then create a picture that fits your point of view.
2. Determine and describe how your client, listener, or prospective buyer fits into the story.
3. Describe why you are there to convey your idea.
4. Describe how your listener will benefit from what you are presenting.
5. Describe how your listener can best use what you are offering.
6. Describe the best way for your listener to purchase or implement your offering.
7. Reiterate the specific benefits of buying and using or implementing what you are offering.

Rules for Storytelling Selling

- Research.
- See through the eye of the beholder.
- Create pictures with your words.
- Create a bridge from the familiar to the new.
- Rehearse.
- Keep it short.

✐ LESSON 7 ✐

Give your all at the outset and something extra along the way. Over time, success will be easier than failure.

Ten "Something Extra" Ideas

1. Do what you're supposed to do.
2. Maintain integrity.
3. Provide an extra service.
4. Offer information.
5. Become an expert.
6. Stay current.
7. Keep training.
8. Offer introductions and contacts.
9. Stay consistent.
10. Be generous.

✐ LESSON 8 ✐

There will always be people who have more experience or skills than you do. If you seek them out as mentors and give back to them in return, they will help you reach your goals.

How to Find a Mentor

- Reach out in writing.
- Attend networking meetings.

- Assist at work.
- Volunteer.
- Rent a mentor.
- Follow role models.

A good mentor:

- Has a track record of success and more experience than you do in the area in which you need mentoring.
- Is willing to listen and actually hear what you are saying.
- Has no blind spot when it comes to you, and is willing to give you unvarnished, truthful perceptions and advice about what steps you must take to reach your goals.
- Is kind and caring but will not do your work for you.
- Expects you to follow up on any advice given, even if you decide for some reason not to take it.
- Gives you a deadline for your step-by-step plan, and stays in touch along the way to see that you've taken those steps.
- Is patient with the process of your growth.
- Recognizes that the hardest part of anything is getting started, and challenges you to take the steps you need to take to get your progress under way.
- Has faith in you, and lets you know he or she believes in you.

How to Keep a Mentor

- Do your homework.
- Send information that might be helpful to your mentor.
- Defend your mentor's good name.
- Always look for big and little ways to say "thank you."
- Acknowledge your mentor in every step of your success.

⊸ LESSON 9 ⊷

Career satisfaction and security depend not on the type of work you do, but on the people you work with and the people you serve.

How to Choose a Career You'll Love

You'll be more satisfied and enjoy greater career security if you choose your career based on the people you'll be working with, not solely on the subject matter that interests you. When considering a career arena, match your skills to an industry that is populated by the types of people you'd love to work with and get to know throughout your career. Jobs aren't consistent, but people are.

When considering a career move, ask yourself:

- What types of people do I want to spend a professional lifetime with?

181

- What types of services could I provide to these people?

Find out if any new job prospect will be a fit by asking:

- What is the dress code? (Do I see myself dressed in The Gap or in St. John knits?)
- Who are the people I'd interact with? (Are these people I can't wait to know?)
- What is the means of interaction? (Interdepartmental meetings? Out of the office with clients? Working on a tight-knit team or toiling quietly away in a cube?)
- What are the day-to-day tasks? (Complex, long-term projects? Simple and predictable?)
- What is the culture of this business? (Big corporation with loads of support? Small, scrappy, and entrepreneurial? Round the clock and lunch at your desk, or nine-to-five and out the door? Hierarchical or collaborative?)

What constitutes a fit for you will likely change as family obligations and other life circumstances change. By choosing carefully based on the community of people you work with, however, you'll be supported as you move seamlessly into positions that fit your position in life.

For expanded exercises on each of *The Golden Apple*'s lessons or to connect with Kathy Aaronson, please go to www.salesathlete.com/goldenapple.

About the Author

Kathy Aaronson is the founder and chief executive officer of The Sales Athlete, Inc. Aaronson took her "bestseller" produce-stand practices all the way to Madison Avenue. She also took with her a principled and dedicated philosophy of identifying and solving problems for the clients she met as she built a highlight-filled career in advertising sales and sales management at *Cosmopolitan*, *Girl Talk*, *W*, *Working Woman*, and McFadden, before turning her full-time focus to The Sales Athlete, Inc.

Executive Search

Sales, marketing, and management executive search is the focus of The Sales Athlete, Inc. Since 1971, The Sales

Athlete, Inc., has worked closely with candidates and client companies, completing thousands of successful assignments nationwide. The Sales Athlete, Inc., enjoys a rich history as a valued resource for success-driven hiring managers who want to hire and retain best-in-market, disciplined, and committed sales and marketing teams.

Training

The Sales Athlete, Inc., also provides training programs on all matters related to hiring, compensating, and retaining top sales, marketing, advertising, and management talent. Aaronson is responsible for having facilitated more than five hundred thousand experienced and inexperienced sales executives coast to coast since 1971.

The Golden Apple Expanded Exercises

For expanded exercises on each of *The Golden Apple*'s lessons, please go to www.salesathlete.com/goldenapple.

For more information about Kathy and The Sales Athlete, Inc., please contact:

KathyAaronson@salesathlete.com
The Sales Athlete, Inc.
9903 Santa Monica Blvd. #2000
Beverly Hills, CA 90212
http://www.salesathlete.com

Index

Index

Bush, George (H. W.), 42
"Business Entertaining" class, 92
business entertainment, 90–92
business experience, in
    childhood, 165–166
buying, looking vs., 3

career coaches, 146–147
career satisfaction and security:
  and authority, 19, 154–164
  building niche careers, 163
  and changes in profession,
    156–157
  and customer relationships,
    60–61
  and professional relationships,
    156–160, 164–165
  questions for evaluating,
    160–161
  and recommendations for jobs,
    162
Cartier, 57
Casual Fridays, 89–90
childhood, business experience
    in, 165–166
clothing. *See* dress
coaches, career, 146–147
commitment:
  to excellence, 130–132
  to training, 136–137
communication:
  with indefinite prospects,
    78–80
  with indifferent prospects,
    72–74
  with interested prospects,
    76–78

misunderstandings in, 121
  as negotiation, 94
  with objectors, 80–82
  with prospects, 66–68
  with rude prospects, 69–72
  with skeptics, 74–76
connection, need for, 154
consistency, 138–139
contacts, offering, 138
corporate culture, 26, 159
Cosmopolitan, 34–36, 104–105, 108
cost-focused customers, 56–58
creating receptivity, 30–37. *See
    also* five-touch technique;
    speed bumps
  with appearance, 88
  importance of, 34
  for new ideas, 103–105
  steps in, 32–33
  with storytelling selling,
    101–103
credibility, 19–20, 25–26
  and behavior/appearance
    outside of business hours, 87
  and consistency, 138–139
  and dress, 88
  and expertise, 135
  and offering contacts, 138
  and packaging, 87, 96
  and regularity of training, 136
  with skeptical prospects, 75–76
  social, 90–94
  from staying current, 136
culture (business), 26, 161
current information, 135–136
customers, 3, 50–61. *See also*
    prospective customers

186

Index

Index

Index

Index